AN & i

Ali North

AN & i

Vanguard Press

VANGUARD PAPERBACK

© Copyright 2018
Ali North

The right of Ali North to be identified as author of
this work has been asserted by her in accordance with the
Copyright, Designs and Patents Act 1988.

All Rights Reserved

No reproduction, copy or transmission of this publication
may be made without written permission.
No paragraph of this publication may be reproduced,
copied or transmitted save with the written permission of the
publisher, or in accordance with the provisions
of the Copyright Act 1956 (as amended).

Any person who commits any unauthorised act in relation to
this publication may be liable to criminal
prosecution and civil claims for damages.

Names of people and identifying places within the book have been
changed to protect the privacy of individuals.

A CIP catalogue record for this title is
available from the British Library.

ISBN 978 1 784653 03 3

Vanguard Press is an imprint of
Pegasus Elliot MacKenzie Publishers Ltd.
www.pegasuspublishers.com

First Published in 2018

Vanguard Press
Sheraton House Castle Park
Cambridge England

Printed & bound in Great Britain

Dedication

I would like to dedicate this book to all those who have suffered from and lost their 'lives' to anorexia nervosa.

Acknowledgements

I would like to thank all the doctors, psychiatrists, psychologists and medical staff that have helped me over the years throughout this battle. I am not exaggerating by saying I would not be here today if it was not for them. However, special thanks must go to Dr C. Adams and Dr W. Mowlds.

Of course my deepest gratitude and love to my family and friends for being there through it all cannot be expressed enough.

CONTENTS

PART I 11
- WELCOME! 13
- MAPLE LANE 14
- DUNLUCE ESTATE 22
- DAD 23
- DARK DAYS 27
- MUM 36
- MR & MRS 38
- PRIMARY SCHOOLDAYS 42
- THE GREAT ESCAPE 43
- AND SO IT BEGAN 59
- MY SECRET FRIEND 75
- UNIVERSITY LIFE 93
- DR ADAMS 104
- WINDSOR HOUSE 106
- UNIVERSITY – SECOND YEAR 114
- CAR ACCIDENT 115
- BELGIUM 118
- FINAL YEAR 131
- WEDDING BELLS 134
- MARRIED LIFE 136
- WHEN HARRY MET… 148
- THE LEAVING 152
- HARRY'S DAD 156
- THE WAITING GAME 161
- THE NEW ARRIVAL 164
- FAMILY LIFE 169
- BREAKDOWN 176
- TRIAL AND ERROR 183

WHERE AM I NOW?......................................186
REGRETS?..187
WHAT NEXT FOR ME?..............................188
PART II..189
WHY ME?...191
WHAT IS AN EATING DISORDER?..........191
ANOREXIA NERVOSA 194
HISTORY OF THE DEADLY DISEASE......195
WHY DOES SOMEONE DEVELOP ANOREXIA NERVOSA ?.............................197
HELP AVAILABLE 198
Physical Treatment 198
Psychiatric treatment 199
Therapies 200
Schema Therapy 201
Self-help..209
Useful Websites...210
MENTAL ILLNESS IN THE UK..................212
THE STORY IN NORTHERN IRELAND.....215
THE FUTURE...218
WHAT NEXT FOR YOU? 219
MY ADVICE?..220
BIBLIOGRAPHY 224

PART I

WELCOME!

Hi there! My name is Alison North, usually just called Ali.

I am a mother, a wife, a daughter, a sister, an aunt, a nanny, a cousin, a friend, a neighbour, an employee… you get my drift? Oh yes and did I say I am also a worthless, horrible piece of dirt! Yip… that is what I said…..a waste of space or so I keep being told!

You see I have another side, my secret friend, an evil part of me who is nasty, a real bitch, who doesn't like me very much – in fact she is extremely cruel, insults me, treats me like filth, denies me food and the most basic needs. She wants to see me suffer and go without – maybe even die – the ultimate sacrifice. But at the same time she wants me to be the most perfect person in the world! Impeccable in everything I say and do. The perfectionist, the ultimate people-pleaser…

But how could this be, you ask?

Welcome to the world of anorexia nervosa – an unbearable life of mental and physical torture. You see in your mind there are two people; one of them a controlling, manipulative secretive tyrant who cannot be seen nor heard by others because she is only known to the anorexic; and the other is the victim – the small, vulnerable child, helpless but trying to survive as best they can. This horrible person tells you what to do all the time, she controls your every thought, word and deed, and you obey but at a price! She is the enemy, your worst nightmare – and that is what this is all about – living hell.

This is my true story…

MAPLE LANE

My first memories as a child, well if you are ever really sure of your first memories, are probably of when I was about four years old. I lived in 30 Maple Lane, a terraced house in a council estate in Ballydunn. Our house had three bedrooms, kitchen, sitting room, front and back small garden and the coal shed! You will hear more about that coal shed later. Home was comfortable enough I thought; it had all the basics and I had my own bedroom. I do not remember much about my own room, there were no personal TVs or hi-tech gadgets in those days but it was fine, I guess. My favourite toy was my dolly Thumbelina, who I adored. At that time, Maple Lane was home to my mum, dad and the youngest of my two brothers, Jack and John. You see, I was the baby of seven kids so by the time I came along the older ones - two brothers, Robert and Samuel, and my older sister, Susan, had left the nest and it was only us youngest three left at home. Sadly, my other sister, Grace, had passed away from a failing heart condition when she was eleven years old. She was called to a higher place on 30 December 1969, now buried alongside my dad in a dark, cold cemetery in our home town. I was only nine months old at the time so I have no living memories of her. I have one photo to this day and occasionally my siblings would mention her. I think in my younger days I looked at bit like her with the same red locks and freckles.

    I think I was a happy enough child in the early years; I suppose I didn't really know what really was going on at that stage. I went to Millfield Primary School and I loved it. I wore a cute maroon pinafore and maroon and gold sash, very smart for a primary school in the early seventies in troubled Northern Ireland that is for sure! But it was a bit strange because my mum worked there as a dinner lady for as long as I can remember. She wore a horrible dark green apron dress and would mainly help the kids at dinner time – hence the title! So I would sometimes see her at playtime – it was great when you had fallen and just wanted your mum because she wasn't far away. Other times it was a real nuisance as she could watch what I was up to and who I was playing with. I do recall being unhappy at times at school, some of the other kids would tease me. I always had to get free school dinners; all the poor kids got those. I remember once asking if I could bring a packed lunch for a change but my dad said it cost too much! The worst times were in Primary 6 and 7, when the school trips came around. I hated that. We never had enough money to even put enough food on the table so school trips were out of the question. So me, and a few others in similar financial dire straits, and I ain't talking about the band, had to stay behind at school and do the 'special jobs' while the others went to places like the zoo or Dublin; it was awful! Everyone knew you didn't have enough money and looked down on me, or so I thought!

I think I must have started realising times were tough at home when I was about six or seven really; a few different memories start to zoom in despite constant efforts to waft them away! I distinctly recall never having a snack at 'break'; in those days there was the obligatory government-paid for (yes really!) teensy weensy bottle of milk; you might have been the lucky one to get a bottle whose top the birds hadn't pecked off! The bottles were freezing especially in winter and they went down like ice; talk about brain freeze. So along with that lactic cocktail others would have had some sort of snack, a bag of crisps, a biscuit or for the fancy well-to-do ones, maybe an apple or a banana – but I never had anything. I don't recall that I ever felt hungry as such but the one day that sticks in my memory when, for some reason, I had a red Penguin chocolate bar, goodness knows how I got that, my dad must have had a windfall on the horses or done a homer. I thought I was brilliant I was the bee's knees – whatever that really means… It was so delicious and I showed everyone I had a snack for break! That was Primary three. I even remember the classroom to this very day – I think I enjoyed the experience of being normal, or not being pitied, more than the actual Penguin!

I was a bright child, always coming top of my classes all through primary school. Each year the top three school kids would receive a prize book at a special Prize Day ceremony and each year I was up there getting a book I had previously picked. I always chose fairy tales with happy endings because I really did want to believe in Happy Ever After! I felt so special, not that my family saw – I don't think they always came to see me.

I also remember us having a family dog. Oh I must have been really young; three or four perhaps. It was a cross between an Alsatian and Collie I think – really a mongrel but special to us. Anyway, it was black and white and called, wait for it, Flicker – now these days a *Flicker* is something different entirely but back then my Flicker was not a scooter, he was my friend. However, being only young, I couldn't always pronounce my words properly and so, much to everyone's humour, I called it

Fucker. So you can imagine the giggles in our street when I would call it for dinner. However, my dad, I haven't mentioned him too much yet, oh that will come – never saw the funny side of that. In fact, when the Minister would come to visit, not that he did much, we were not devout Christians or anything, but sometimes my dad would go through a religious phase and we would all have to go to church and have the Minister around to ours for tea. So when the Minister would be about to visit my dad would say, 'hide her or hide that bloody dog!' Think it was normally me that was hidden! My dad could make excuses for the dog.

    I remember family visiting sometimes but not too often. One funny story which sticks in my head was when my really posh aunt, Mum's sister, my Aunt Loretta, called to visit with her husband and my granny. I always remember when we went to her house we were on strict instructions from my dad not to go near her glass ornaments – she had a glass table full of about twenty coloured glass ornaments, polished daily and they took pride of place in her sitting room! God help us if we even looked towards the table. So this posh aunt, accustomed to the best of china, called to ours, and as usually happens, visitors get a cup of tea and a wee biscuit. Well, my aunt would have been looking down on our everyday dishware at the best of times but she wasn't prepared for what she got! At four, I insisted our guests got tea from my tea set too, yes the one that I had been playing in the garden with not an hour previously, and oh no it wasn't a pretend tea party I wanted to do it right so I sneakily went into the kitchen and filled three of my wee, dirty teacups full of real tea and proceeded to serve our guests! I think there may even have been a blade or two of grass hanging out the side of the cup I served to my Aunt Loretta! Well her face was a sight for sore eyes… funny she didn't visit much after that!

I have been told that my parents used to go dancing on a Saturday night and I was left in the supposed care of Jack and John. Well, that was not the smartest idea my dad ever had, but he would probably have done anything to get out for a drink and my mum knew she had to go with him to keep an eye on him. So, no choice I suppose. Anyway, when I was older my brothers used to take great pleasure in telling me that the minute my parents walked out the front door they opened the back door and sent me packing to the coal shed for the evening. I am not saying they were sadistically cruel or anything but they just didn't want me in the house to spoil their fun. I was just a nuisance to them. So off I would go with my favourite doll, Thumbelina, which they had also destroyed. Her hair had been cut and not with finesse and they had scribbled all over her face. But the worst bit was that she had a string in her back which, when pulled, made her sing the sweetest song "Thumbelina, Thumbelina…" Well, that had been pulled out too! My Thumbelina was now dumb as well! But I still loved her, a bit like Bagpuss, "a saggy old cloth cat, baggy, and a bit loose at the seams, but Emily loved him!"

I mentioned before that my older brothers and sister no longer lived at home when I was growing up. In fact they had all left home. You see, in the early seventies in Northern Ireland the infamous "Troubles" had started. Innocent people were being murdered by bullets and bombs. It was not a nice country to grow up in.

So the second eldest, Robert, decided to get away from it all and emigrate to Canada which in those days was like going to the Moon! Some people had heard of it but no one actually knew anyone who had gone there! And he went on his own. I do not remember his leaving as I was really young. However, after he had settled and was starting to enjoy his new life in Canada playing Davy Crockett, he wrote home – yes, remember those things called letters (no texts, Whatsapp or Facebook in those days) and suggested my eldest brother, wife and their two young sons emigrate out there too for a better life.

Sorry, did I forget to mention I was an aunt – yip, in fact I had been an Aunt since I was only six weeks old! Yes many funny stories abound on that – my sister, about sixteen when Jacob (the first nephew) and I were born, used to take us both out in the one pram, as I said times were hard in those days, and people would stop and say, "Aw your wee brother and sister." And she would correct them and say, well actually, pointing to me, a little baby, "She is his aunt!"

My sister was very good to us both. I vaguely remember her taking Jacob and I to the cinema for the very first time; or to the 'pictures' as we said in those days. It was to see *Snow White and the Seven Dwarfs*. I think we must have been about four. She said the minute all the lights went out and the movie was about to start, the surprise of the sudden darkness forced me to call out in my loudest voice, "Hey Jacob can you see me? I can't see you. Can you see me?" My sister said everyone in the cinema was in stitches at us. This just made the matter funnier as the louder everyone laughed, the louder I had to call out!

So back to the story: that is what they did – my eldest brother and his family emigrated to Canada too; to

Vancouver to be precise, a big city on the west coast of Canada in the state of British Columbia.

Now I do recall snippets of the morning they left. I think I was about four and had already started primary school. They left very early in the morning from our house to go to the airport and I remember seeing them off. My sister-in-law gave me a beautiful brown leather coin purse and then, after they left, I remember being really early for school. That was the extent of my memories of their no-doubt tearful departure.

During the first few years after both brothers emigrated we heard a little from them by way of letters and the odd Christmas present. Years later with the arrival of a house phone – that was when we had enough money to have one installed – we received the occasional phone call again, usually at Christmases or birthdays.

And my brothers are still in Vancouver. Returning more often in later years with the advance in air travel and to celebrate the expansion of the family circle and share special occasions, especially Mum's milestone birthdays. As I write she has just turned eighty-six!

After a few years of my brothers' exodus to pastures new, my sister too decided to leave Northern Ireland behind and ventured first to England to train as a nurse and then, many years thereafter, to Scotland to teach. Being slightly closer to home she would have occasionally travelled back by ferry in the later years and she always sent presents. I recall once being told I was getting a special gift and dad and I had to go to the post-office depot to collect it. There were no special delivery services in those days. I was thrilled. We went up and down to the depot for several days each time, coming home disappointed as the package still had not arrived.

Then one day when we called up they presented us with this, what seemed like a massive box, I was so excited. When we got it home I opened it up to find a red leather twin doll's pram. Wow! First of its kind, I had never seen a twin pram before. And my sister had made me twin pillows and blanket sets to match. She was, and still is ever so good to me. I think as she was in her teens when Jack, John and I were growing up she maybe behaved more like a mummy than a sister to us at times. I loved the pram and I used to pile all my dollies into it. Now a funny thing happened. That Christmas Santa obviously decided I needed proper twin dolls to put in my twin pram. So that Christmas morning I remember coming down to open a very unusual Christmas present – twin dolls but twin dolls with a difference – they were special – one was white and one was black! I was five at the time and knew nothing about racism or discrimination but I hated that black doll. I had never seen a black doll before and just thought she looked dirty. So when I would go out to play, I always put the blanket over her face and told everyone not to look at her she was sleeping! Bless the child…

DUNLUCE ESTATE

Then I remember one Sunday Mum, Dad and I went out for a walk – now this was a rare occurrence. For one, Dad didn't usually do Sundays; he was either still AWOL from a drunken weekend or if he was home he was in bed with a serious hangover! So I do recall this walk quite vividly. We walked quite a bit; it was a lovely sunny day and we ended up walking through a new council housing development in another part of the town. In my young innocence I thought the house was gorgeous, all new and really bright and clean. Little did I know for some reason Mum or Dad, maybe both, had asked to move house and we had been allocated this one. That's how it worked. Obviously I had not known about any of this beforehand. So we upped sticks and moved. It all seemed exciting for a while, we brought most of the old furniture with us and although the house was no bigger I do remember we had a separate toilet and bathroom, always useful! I would have been about seven or so by this stage and so my memories are more vivid. Unfortunately, I started to become more aware of our family circumstances. First of all, money was scarce, as I mentioned before, Mum worked in the school as a dinner lady so only a few pounds coming in from that. And secondly, Mum and Dad argued a lot.

DAD

In my early years I never recall if my dad worked. Then in the later primary school days I know he did a bit. He worked as a fitter, a tradesman. I remember him working with a few other guys from Bangor and Belfast, about fifty/sixty miles away from ours. To me then that was awesome, so far away. I had never been to either of those places. There were three from the Belfast area, all from the same family, the dad, Victor, and two sons, David and Peter. They often stayed in a guest house in the town to be near to the job and save the sixty mile journey up and down every day. So my dad worked with these men as part of a team on a big job at Magilligan prison, on the north coast of Northern Ireland about twenty-five miles from the Giant's Causeway. Magilligan is still an infamous prison in Northern Ireland today. Now a few things stick in my head particularly about my dad working with these men. One day, when I was walking in the school line to dinners, I saw Dad's workmates standing at the entrance to my school, but my dad was not with them. It seemed a bit odd but I never really thought too much more of it at the time. Shortly after that I found out they had come to fetch my mum because Dad had suffered a heart attack at work. Dad wasn't able to work for a long time after that. In fact, I think that was his last real job!

But even after my dad stopped working with these guys they still kept in touch, one in particular; David. In fact he started coming down and staying at weekends and special occasions. We would all go out to a bar in

Magilligan called the Mallard – it was old-fashioned stuff, there would be a Country and Western band playing in a big hall and then during the break they would play bingo or Mr and Mrs. I thought it was great fun. I was about eight or nine and in those days it was totally fine for kids to be running around those types of establishments. I would wander about, play the fruit machines and have crisps. Meanwhile the adults would have a wee dance and a few drinks (in my Dad's case) and since David didn't really drink he would drive us out and in; so no need for a taxi or babysitter. It was brilliant, and very good of him, I thought! This turned out to have great significance on the rest of my life as you will soon learn!

I know in later years, even though Dad was never formally employed again, he did a few 'homers' – painting and decorating for people – on the quiet of course! He was good at DIY stuff, you see he was a perfectionist and so every piece of work was like a masterpiece, Michelangelo would have been proud. But generally the next few years I mostly remember Dad out of work, claiming the dole or the "bru" as it is also known in Northern Ireland. Then, as regular as clockwork, he would wait outside my school every Friday to meet Mum as she had just got paid! We wouldn't probably see him again for days. He spent a lot of time in the pubs, his local was Rabbie's – named after the owner, a former football player for the local town. The rest of the time he was home drunk and that is where the memories aren't so nice.

Some days I would come home from school and Mum would be crying and Dad would be dressed to kill, not literally of course but I mean looking very dapper or in the words of Meatloaf – 'All dressed up and no place to go'. I suppose it was his army background, hat, shirt and tie, polished shoes – no sloppy gear in our house! I always guessed the story: Dad was asking Mum for money, Mum said she had none, and he would keep on guessing she had a few pence literally put away from child benefit or something. Eventually if Mum had any she would just give it to him to get peace and get rid of him for a while. Other times if she was really penniless, which was often the case, he would just go anyway and I can only guess that he borrowed from some of the other drunken cronies or he had a tab at Rabbie's. Either way he would leave and we wouldn't see him again until the money had ran out and he would come home drunk and aggressive, whether that was a few hours or days later, most often the latter.

That type of dad and lifestyle was what I was used to. In fact, when I heard the Boomtown Rats single *'I Don't Like Mondays',* a big hit in 1979, I honestly thought it was about the cheap wine (Mundy's, similar to Buckfast nowadays). To me all that was normal life. I didn't know any different, but that was soon to change as I grew up and saw and heard more!

All this time there was no obvious sign that I was suffering from any mental illness or eating disorder. What I and others did not know was that the seeds had been planted.

In later years I learnt that dad had fought in the Second World War – in Palestine. I have his service medals to this day. He had lied about his age and enlisted when he was just sixteen for queen and country. That is where the troubled mind probably stems. Drinking and smoking was a way of life for soldiers then – that was their solace. They saw and lived a hard life and for many, like my dad, they came home with post-traumatic stress disorder, although it was neither diagnosed nor treated back then. But many men, just like soldiers of today, are mentally scarred and can never be the same again. Dad brought his terror home with him and learnt to drown his sorrows in a bottle of whiskey and then vent his anger for the past on my mum and us. My dad was most likely clinically depressed. His life after returning from war was tarnished – he had blood on his hands, which he could never wash off and we paid the price.

DARK DAYS

I do not know if I was just getting older or wiser or whether Dad's drinking actually got worse. My childhood memories from that stage in my life are dominated by my dad's drunken behaviour. I don't remember too much about the days, it was the nights that haunt me. And it didn't necessarily have to be a Friday or Saturday night that one would usually associate with drinking: it could have been, and often was, any night of the week. But what I haven't mentioned yet is that the problem did not stop at the drink. Sadly, the consequence of the drink was the violence; the violent behaviour against all of us but mainly on Mum. She became a punchbag in every physical and mental way possible.

And this is where I come in, literally. I used to try to protect her; I tried to save her from my dad. I tried to make him see sense but it was futile. But that didn't stop me trying. When Dad was out drinking at bedtime Mum and I would snuggle into my bed hoping and praying he just wouldn't come home. Now Mum never really said that but I know we were both thinking it. But neither of us really settled, we were half sleeping, half listening out for the key turning in the lock or the knock at the door if he had once again lost his key. He would immediately bellow my mum's name and usually demand she get up and make him something to eat, no matter what time it was or the fact that his kids were in bed. Sometimes she got up straight away when he staggered home just for an easy life. If she didn't, I knew after he stumbled upstairs looking into their bedroom for her and, seeing she wasn't there, he would storm into my room and yell for her to get into her own bed. I would tell her to pretend she was sleeping, stupidly trying to convince both of us that Dad would leave us in peace. I would lie shaking with my eyes closed tight; dreading the minute my dad would burst through the door in rage shouting for my mum. I would try and intervene and tell Dad to keep quiet, Mum was sleeping and to leave her alone but it was useless. Despite my valiant efforts I couldn't protect Mum. I was a wee girl and I was trying to be Mum's bodyguard from this 'animal' but I failed. He would just yell all the louder and physically try to drag Mum from my bed. This made me cry and scream even louder, holding desperately onto Mum as I knew what he would do to her if he got her into their room. And unfortunately that is exactly what happened.

    I begged and pleaded for him to stop and leave her alone, but he just ignored me or hit me for getting in the way and I would be ordered back to my bed and to stay in my room. I would cry myself to sleep, hoping and praying for him to stop beating her; sometimes I eventually fell over to sleep. Other nights I watched the dawn rise gradually feeling calmer when all fell silent. As morning came whether from slumber or a sleepless night I was often eager but scared to see Mum to check if she was OK.

    Sometimes he was careless and the bruises were clear to see on Mum's face or lower arms, but most of the time he was crafty and they were well hidden under her clothes. But she could never hide the pain in her eyes and the worn, desperate look in her face. That became the norm. That became my norm. I saw my life as trying to be there for Mum, scared to leave her. I had to try to please her and Dad, doing anything possible to save the situation or make them happy with me at least, if not with each other!

One time Mum took really ill, on and off for weeks, often in writhing pain. It turned out she had gallstones and had to go into hospital to have them removed. Twice she was admitted for potential surgery but on both occasions the doctors refused to operate as she was so badly beaten.

One of the saddest things back then was that neither the Police nor medical staff did anything about physical abuse between spouses. They didn't want to get involved. Thankfully it is not like that today! So my dad had free rein to treat my mum like dirt without consequence. Many a night my dad was attacking my mum so badly that I would run into the street in the hope that some passers-by would help me stop him, but no. I was about eight or nine at this stage. No-one wanted to know in those days. No-one wanted to risk coming between a man and his wife especially when the man was my dad. Not many would be stepping forward to challenge him, let's say!

I usually remember just Mum and me in the house most nights. I do not remember Jack or John being at home much. They were in their teens by then and usually still out when my dad came home. Other nights they were in bed, out for the count and slept through it all – or at least pretended to. You see they shared the bedroom at the back of the house whereas my wee room was right beside Mum and Dad's at the front. However, one particular night will stay with me forever. My brothers were in bed when Dad staggered home ready for the usual night's brawl. I can still vividly picture the scene. Dad had come upstairs to look for Mum and had dragged her from beside me in my bed. I ran after her screaming, begging him to leave her alone. My older brother Jack came out of his bedroom and tried to stop Dad from attacking Mum. Suddenly Dad turned on him and grabbed him by the throat with his tightened fist, his face enraged that one of his sons had dared stand up to him. Mum was screaming trying to pull Dad off Jack. Terrified, I ran downstairs into the street as I heard some men walking by and begged them to come in and help me, but they didn't want to know. All I remember was a lot of screaming. I do not know how my brother survived that night but he did; well physically anyway. The next morning he moved out. He was only eighteen. I couldn't help my brother, either.

No-one has ever mentioned that night since. Another horror story locked away.

Sometimes my dad would disappear for days on end and we wouldn't know where he was. We never really knew where Dad got money to drink so much. He wasn't working. Mum had very little and needed to pay for everything. Once he vanished for about a week or so. We honestly thought he had gone for good. I remember secretly feeling so happy and relieved. Each day without him brought a little bit more hope that he was away for good. A part of me felt guilty for having such feelings but I couldn't help it. I started to imagine how peaceful and more relaxed life could be without Dad around. Mum and I were just getting settled to watch TV on the Saturday night – it was summer, kids were out playing in the grass in front and looking back I genuinely think I felt so happy. Not a care in the world and at that stage I actually hoped Dad would never come back. It was just so much easier when he wasn't around. Then… I saw him, staggering up the street in front of my friends and our neighbours. I just felt my heart breaking. First, I felt so embarrassed he was so drunk and couldn't even walk straight. The short-lived happiness was over and immediately the fear of what the night would bring drew a shadow over Mum and I. We just sat there numb, waiting for him to fall in the door. Months later Mum found out that Dad had visited my granny and grandad, Mum's parents, before he had gone AWOL. Apparently he told them he would leave us alone and never return home if they gave him money – so they did, he took quite a bit of money from those two pensioners who would do anything to save us from him. But what did he do – he blew it drinking for a week, then came back!

My dad never troubled his own parents in that way, you see my paternal grandparents lived in Portlouth and we would only visit them a few times a year. Their house wasn't within walking distance and we didn't have a car for most of my childhood. So we would make the trip by train in the better weather or maybe sometimes my uncle would call and take us there. I have very vivid memories of their house. It was a three-storey town house, very grand. It always felt very warm and welcoming with a couple of coal fires going all the time. However, the set-up was far from normal. You see, my Granny Acheson had had a stroke before I was born and I always remember her lying in a great big bed in the front sitting room by the large bay window. She would always be dressed like the Queen Mother, wearing the most elegant bed wear; beautiful linen nightdresses, lace bed shawls, a hair bonnet bejeweled with diamond brooches and her expensive rings. She always wore a pearl necklace too.

From waist down she was covered by fancy bedlinen and blankets. She looked amazing and she was a well-known figure in the area. Everyone would walk or drive by and wave in and many local celebrities would pop in and have a wee cuppa with her. Everyone knew my Granny Acheson. We used to love going to see her. Even though she couldn't walk nor talk, we would sit beside her and hold her hand and chat away to her. She would just smile and nod in recognition. Granny was so sweet. And my grandad Acheson would sit nearby all day long by the fireside smoking his pipe and chatting away to his beloved. My grandad was another special character; he had fought in the First World War and had many stories to tell. My Aunt Winnie, my dad's sister, devoted her life to looking after my grandparents. She lived with them and cared selflessly for their every need. She was a frail wee woman but fierce; you didn't mess with my Aunt Winnie and she wouldn't hold back telling you what she thought either! But she was very kind to us. We used to love going to visit my grandparents particularly as my Aunt Winnie would put on a lavish banquet any time there were visitors. There would be freshly baked bread, scones and homemade cakes and biscuits. We loved it! We never had much fancy food at home and we often felt hungry. Cakes and buns were a rarity and you definitely wouldn't have had your five a day in our house!

Funny story: one day Mum had been paid and went to the local shop to stock up with a few things. There were no major supermarkets like nowadays. Most people just shopped in their local stores. This one time she came back with some fresh apples and she put them into our fruit bowl, which was normally home to plastic fruit – why would you do that? Anyway, we hadn't had fresh fruit in months probably so my brother and I took one immediately and after another wee while thought we would eat another one, so after a few hours they had all gone. My Mum was furious and turned to us and said, "Why did you eat those apples so quickly, do you think apples grow on trees?"

To Granny and Grandad Acheson and my Aunt Winnie my dad was an angel, or if they knew any different they certainly weren't letting on.

Sometimes my dad would be supposed to do a job or a favour for someone and he would disappear and let them down. Or he would arrive just in time but drunk. I remember a few times when my sister was coming home from Scotland by ferry and Dad was supposed to go and collect her from Larne in a borrowed car: he would show up about an hour before he was due to leave but totally plastered. So, on the few occasions that Dad was reasonably calm and not too aggressive, Mum would coax him to go and lie down on the sofa for a nap. Then she would wake him with a strong cup of tea, a few painkillers and then pack him in the car to get my sister. But not only that, she would make me go with him! Yip, you heard right, she sent my drunk father off in the car to fetch my sister and, thinking I would stop him from going into a pub along the way, she sent me too! I don't know if she thought of the potential danger in that plan or if she just stupidly thought that was the best idea! I honestly do not know how we both survived those journeys, I had to keep my eyes glued to the road and my hand on the steering wheel in case Dad nodded off – it was a nightmare! If we had ever been involved in an accident or if my dad had been stopped by the Police he would have been in serious trouble. It was a wonder no-one was ever killed. Again, I got used to my role as go-between, mediator, trying to protect everyone from harm.

Many a time, day and night, not only did my dad arrive home drunk but he would bring a few other local alcoholics home with him too, maybe to stay for a few hours while Mum had to make them all some food before they headed out again or sometimes they slept on the sofa. So some mornings I came down to a fuller house than usual. I was taught very early on in life how to make my dad his 'cure' – raw eggs, milk and sugar, to set him up on his way again.

I had a few friends around where we lived and sometimes, as wee girls do, you like to have sleepovers. The only problem was this was a double-edged sword for me – I wanted to have and do the normal things, like invite friends over to stay, but I was terrified in case my dad got drunk and started his usual behaviour. So I never had friends to stay at my house. Then if friends invited me to stay at their house, the same dilemma occurred: I wanted to go and have fun but was petrified of what might happen to Mum if I wasn't there to protect her. So that never really happened either. While I knew I couldn't always stop Dad from hurting Mum I knew at least I had to try. If I wasn't there I was scared of what the consequences might be. And then what if it was too late!

I do not really remember any family holidays as such. And we didn't really go on days out together either due to no money or no Dad! However, I do recall one summer going for a week to Butlins just outside Dublin – we had just got a cheap car, a red Morris Minor 1300. But I thought we were cool, at last we had some wheels! So we had a week in Butlins, I remember the chalet, very small, cramped and basic but back then I thought it was brilliant. I remember we all went and ate in a big canteen-like hall. There were different events going on during the day such as kids' activities – I remember some amusements and the Puffin' Billy train. At night, there were things like bingo and one night my mum won the Glamorous Granny competition. However, my most vivid memory from that trip was the night we were walking back to our chalet passed the Bingo Hall. Mum, Dad and I were walking along leisurely and Jack and John were running ahead. As we approached the Bingo Hall entrance doors all I heard was someone calling "Full House!" and the sound of everyone sighing because they hadn't won, and the scraping of chairs as they got up to leave. The next thing I noticed were my naughty brothers running at speed up ahead laughing hysterically! It didn't take long for my astute father to put two and two together – Jack had opened the door and shouted "Full House!" and ran! Well, my Dad battered him sore that night, it is a wonder we weren't thrown out of Butlins. That is my only holiday memory as a family. Maybe that is one of the reason I love travelling so much now…

MUM

It is quite strange but my memories of Mum are quite few, or rather I should say the types of memories do not differ greatly. If someone was to ask me immediately about my mum back then it would be of a sad, cross woman in a green overall – you see that was her dinner lady uniform at my school. I always remember her at the other end of my dad's anger and fists – she was always the victim – it is as if she did not have any identity of her own. She was always the appendage to my dad and not in a good way. I do remember her as very hardworking either with her part-time jobs here or there or working in the house as my dad was a clean freak! Everything always had to be spotless; I suppose that was the army background coming out in him! She never really had a life of her own, no personal identity, and certainly no social life.

In later years I remember her going to bingo a few nights a week but in the end that wasn't really the case, as you will read later. Mum just always seemed to be down and exasperated with life, including us. Sadly, I do not recall many happy memories of my mum in the early years or if there were any, they were short-lived.

One funny thing I do recall is every Sunday, Dad permitting, Mum would try to get everything done in the house and get herself washed, dressed and some lipstick on to settle down for the big Sunday movie with the lion at the start! That is how she referred to the classic MGM movies shown every Sunday. I do not think she really cared what the film was about. To her it must have represented that hope for a piece of relaxation and rest; possibly escapism. Some Sundays it happened, usually if my dad was AWOL or if he was still hungover in bed. There would often be the usual thump of the floor overhead shouting for us to get him more water or something, but I would usually have done that to allow Mum some peace. I still keep Mum going about the big film with the lion at the start!

Another occasion that sticks in my mind was my sister's engagement party. Usually my relationship with Mum was very matter-of-fact. I don't recall her ever being really fun or overly tactile. She probably did in her own way. It just always felt like Mum didn't have any energy, patience or strength left to deal with my brothers and I. Dad wore her down and so when it came to us, it was all a bit of a struggle I think. Anyway, I once overheard her say to her closest friend that she wouldn't go to my Sister's engagement party in Scotland if I was going. When I heard that I felt broken. I couldn't believe my mum would say such a thing, never mind think like that. I never understood that. I kept thinking she didn't love me and that I must have been a real nuisance. But that's what happened – Mum, Dad, Jack and John went to Glasgow for Susan's engagement party and I stayed all weekend with my mum's friend. Deep inside, although I never said anything, I was really hurt and didn't understand what I had done wrong. Maybe she had her reasons, but I never understood.

MR & MRS

You will not be surprised to read that my memories of Mum and Dad as a couple are largely horrendous, painful. Traumatising in fact. I do not know what they had in common really but sure, you could say that about many a couple even today! I suppose there must have been some attraction when they met in their teens. I think they met at a dance when Dad was back home between army stints. That was one thing they both enjoyed – dancing – proper ballroom dancing, I have seen a few old photos of them dancing away and they seemed surprisingly happy back then. I suppose Dad went away again and then they decided to get married or whatever on his next return home. I realise it was different back then. Soldiers didn't really know what lay ahead of them when they went back to fight so they usually grabbed any opportunity when home for fun when they could. Plus it was the norm for people to marry quite young in those days. Mum and Dad were married on Boxing Day 1948. Nowadays that date may seem quite strange for a wedding but during wartime it was quite usual to find couples being married at holiday times like Boxing Day, Easter Monday as these were most likely times troops might get a visit home. In later years, on those Saturday nights when we used to frequent the Mallard, Mum and Dad would often have had a wee dance or two but the smiles weren't so big or as genuine then. It would usually have been at the order of my dad to show who was boss rather than for their mutual pleasure. They sometimes entered the Mr & Mrs competition but they rarely got matching answers, much to the disgust of my dad.

In fact, although trying very hard I honestly cannot remember one truly happy time with Mum and Dad or witnessing a genuinely good time between them. Dad was always putting Mum down in front of others, criticising her and her so-called stupidity. When it came to schooling and homework time, whenever he was around, he would often joke that there was no point asking your ma coz she wouldn't know! Mum was not very academic, let's say, she just didn't have that educational background and never really paid any attention to our homework or anything. Dad was the brain box in the house and he always let Mum know it.

Even their twenty-fifth wedding anniversary, which you would think would be a happy occasion, turned sour. I remember there being a party in our house and to any child family parties are great. There were lots of people, family and friends coming and going, there was special food and a cake and a so-called happy atmosphere. These types of occasions gave me some sort of inner relief for a bit because I thought the more people were around, the less chance the devil in Dad would make an appearance. I remember one of our neighbours was charged, or else volunteered, to keep an eye on me that night – I think I was about seven or eight and so I was nipping in and out of her house and it was all great fun, I thought. And then I distinctly remember sitting in the corner of our crowded sitting room, the night was getting on and my dad of course had had a few drinks and was starting to sing. I maybe haven't mentioned that yet but, yes my dad was a really good singer. Soldiers, with little to do when away, other than fight for your country of course, they would have entertained themselves. On occasion they maybe had a few drinks and a wee sing-song. Oh, I still recall those wartime songs, mainly romantic as they were about missing loved ones and so on.

Anyway, back to the story: so my dad had started to sing a wee number and was in full swing when I think Mum made a simple comment to Dad to turn around so she could see him sing as his back was to her. That was it. That was all she said – a simple request – nothing more, asked in a pleasant way in front of their visitors there to celebrate their twenty-fifth wedding anniversary. But sadly that was all it took and the night suddenly turned – Dad was furious – he instantly stopped singing, started shouting at Mum, how dare she tell him what to do and Mum instantly burst into tears and, embarrassed and hurt, she left the room. Meanwhile others tried to calm the situation and then almost instantly, as if nothing had happened, Dad went back to singing. He put the fear of God into everyone who felt compelled to sit and listen intently. Despite many wanting to challenge my dad and sympathise with Mum, no one did. Obviously the night had been ruined – Happy 25th Wedding Anniversary – it said it all. That night was symbolic of their relationship: Dad in control and ordering everyone around regardless of how he hurt others.

Looking back, many would say how did they even last twenty-five years but it was very different back then. There weren't the same opportunities or support for women to leave their husbands despite the horrendous abuse they suffered – they were really on their own. And ultimately, you will hear it time and time again, women "stayed for the kids". They thought that was best for them.

One thing was different about that night and which hardly ever happened; Dad showed his nasty side in front of others. In public he always tried to convey the perfect gentleman, the ideal, smart, clever husband and father. He rarely let his guard down – but he did that night!

You will not be surprised to hear then that I have few genuinely happy memories of my dad. But I do have a couple of fleeting ones. When he was sober he would have liked me to comb his hair over, the few strands that were left. And I sometimes, not often, would have been able to cuddle up on the couch beside him. My dad – I did love him so… I enjoyed that little bit of innocent, quiet time with him.

I do recall my dad introducing me to the old BBC2 quiz programme *Call my Bluff* and coffee. I was very educationally-minded like Dad, even at a young age, and together we liked to guess the quiz words – we were both quite intellectual and competitive. And while we watched this Dad made us coffee. It was my first taste of coffee and Dad made it with milk for me in a lovely cup and saucer. That was probably the best quality time I ever had with Dad.

Ironically, those few occasions occurred when Mum was away out at bingo, planning something else!

PRIMARY SCHOOLDAYS

No matter what was going on at home I never let it get in the way of my schoolwork. I loved school. I think subconsciously I saw school as an escape from home life. I had a few wee friends and I would walk the whole way to and from school every morning and afternoon. Quite a distance for a child that age – three miles – but I didn't mind. All the teachers knew me particularly as my mum worked as a dinner lady. Most teachers also knew me through my other siblings as they too had attended Millfield. I think deep down some of them also knew about my dad and probably felt sorry for us! Surprisingly, I did quite well at school, coming top in most subjects every year. I was also in the choir, netball team and in the school play. In fact, I was well on the way to becoming the head girl and getting the 'gold watch' – the esteemed prize awarded to the top pupil in Primary seven before they left for big school. But alas, as you will soon read, the prize wasn't to be mine!

So that was my primary school years. Life then was largely a big secret, I didn't dare ever tell anyone else what was really going on at home. In fact, I actually pretended to myself and others that my life, our family life was the opposite, that all was glorious, that life was great, I even convinced myself, sometimes. You see the pattern forming…

THE GREAT ESCAPE

One of the biggest secrets in my life came while I was in Primary seven, towards the end of 1979. On 7 December 1979 about 6 o'clock at night to be exact. I was ten years and eight months!

First I need to take you back a few weeks or months to set the scene. When Mum got me alone one night in early December she told me a big secret that she stressed I could not tell anyone especially not Dad or I was in big trouble. She told me we were going to run away and a friend was going to take us away to a safe place where Dad could never harm us again. She even told me the date – it was going to be Friday 7 December 1979 around teatime. She said that, from now until then, I had to, bit by bit, pack away toys or books I wanted to take away, but only my favourites as there wasn't room to take everything.

To be quite honest I cannot really remember feeling too much – it was all said very practically. I didn't even try to think who the friend was. I never asked where exactly we were going or how we were getting there. I just did what I was told. So I had to start by deciding which toys to take and which to leave; but I didn't have that much anyway so it wasn't too difficult a decision. And I never mentioned anything to anyone. I didn't even dare raise the matter with Mum unless she spoke of it first. I did not know who knew – I did not know if Mum had told Jack or John or any of the rest of the family. So I kept quiet. I was scared she would go off and leave me.

As the date grew closer I must admit I found the secret really hard to keep. Don't get me wrong, I was never tempted to tell anyone, but it sort of ate away at me – this really big secret. I felt quite scared not knowing what was going to happen and not being allowed to tell anyone. I sort of felt guilty about leaving my dad and my brother; you see John was not coming. Whenever I found it really unbearable I dreamed of where we were going. I imagined a really fancy house, every little girl's dream of a big white house with pillars, fountains, lovely big gardens and a sweeping driveway. Inside would be filled with luxurious furniture and decorated so elegantly. The cupboards would be brimming with loads of fancy food and the wardrobes full of beautiful, new clothes. A fairy tale!

The morning of Friday 7 December 1979 arrived and I went to school as usual. As the day went on I was feeling extremely guilty and anxious; typical but that afternoon I was given responsibility for the netball kit for the whole team as I had been chosen as captain for the school game the following Monday. I had also been given lead role in the school Christmas play and was allowed to take the master script home with me to copy out my lines over the weekend on the sole condition I returned it to school first thing Monday morning. As I was being told all this in school I really felt my heart would break. I couldn't say anything – how could I explain I wouldn't be there on Monday and that after the bell rang at three o'clock I was gone and would never be back? So as home time approached I tried to act as if nothing was wrong and painfully said goodbye to my teacher and my best friends. As they called back see you Monday I just froze; because I knew I wouldn't be there on Monday, or the next day or any day after that. I had a very long, difficult walk home trying to think what I was going to do with the netball kit and the script! How could I sort it out without telling anyone what was about to happen, without telling someone about my big, dirty secret?

When I arrived home Mum was there rushing me to get sorted. I explained I had to nip out and would be back soon. She shouted after me to hurry as it was nearly time to go. So quickly I ran around to one of my best friend's house – luckily the house was in darkness. I recalled they all went swimming on a Friday night – nice family quality time I thought, as I was preparing to flee with one parent to get away from the other – you couldn't really get a more opposite situation, I thought! Anyway I shoved the script through the door with a scribbled note with my name and the word 'Sorry'. I often wonder what Deborah thought when she found it or what was said at school about me on Monday.

Next I ran to another friend's house; she played netball with me. This time the house was all lit up and I could hear kids inside. I quickly rang the doorbell and ran. I had left a similar note with all the netball kit on the doorstep. I felt riddled with guilt and betrayal.

I raced home and Mum was literally waiting at the back door for me. As we were gathering our last bits and pieces up, John – he obviously knew what was going on – ran from the front sitting room to say Dad was coming up the hill! What were the odds – must have been the first Friday night in ages that my dad had actually appeared home at teatime? As I said, John wasn't coming with us, he had just left school a few months before and had started a wee job, so he decided he would stay and try to be there for Dad for the first while as he would be on his own.

Well at that, Mum grabbed my hand and we ran out the backyard and down through the estate not taking a second to look behind. I never knew how my brother told my Dad we had gone or what immediately followed, but I have a pretty good guess.

I always wondered what my friends thought after that night. I am sure they were rather bemused especially when I didn't turn up at school on Monday or ever after.

That night was a real milestone in my life: the end of one chapter and the beginning of another.

Mum and I ran for a good five or ten minutes and then stopped near a power station. Just by that, a red and black car pulled up. It was David – Mum's knight in shining armour. It was all falling into place now like an extremely confusing jigsaw! He had been part of the plan all along. I didn't realise that, or else I chose not to. Things over the past few weeks, even months, were starting to make sense now – all those nights out playing bingo, Mum hadn't been going to play bingo at all. Mum had been going out with him. And all those Saturdays I was left on my own when Mum said she was going out for a special message and I couldn't come – it was him she was going to see. And that Saturday afternoon when I was at home and Jack arrived looking very angry and had words with Mum – he had seen Mum and David in his car – he had asked her what was going on, but I do not know what he ever did about it or if he ever told anyone. It was all buzzing around in my head now.

We quickly got into the car and he drove off. Just like that. As I sat in the car looking out at the darkness for what seemed like an eternity to wherever my new home was going to be, I felt sick; not sure if it was physical or emotional at that stage. It was overwhelming for me. I think the recent events were all just whirling around in my head – I had been literally swept away by Mum, with no choice or ability to think or feel. I was numb. I must have eventually fallen asleep for a while because suddenly I felt the car stop and Mum and David were getting out.

When I got out into the dark night it must have been near nine. I quickly tried to focus my eyes on my new surroundings. We had arrived at a safe house in a small housing area in the countryside called Clough. It was a small pebble-dashed end-of-terrace house. Where were my white pillars and my driveway? When I went inside it just got worse. The house was filled with old second-hand furniture and I felt sick – it wasn't a dream any longer, reality had bitten real hard. I wanted to turn back and pretend it was all a nightmare and I would wake up in my own bed. There was a small kitchen/dining room and a downstairs sitting room. The oddest thing was the bathroom – the only bathroom – was downstairs but you had to go through the kitchen to reach it – don't think it would have passed building control to be honest. Upstairs there were three bedrooms.

The next few days were a bit of a blur really. In those days there was no Internet or Facebook. The only form of communication was by landline telephone or letter. I knew things were going on because Mum was on the phone a few times with my brothers and sister. I overheard her saying that we had been mentioned on the radio as missing persons and the Police were looking for us. So Mum had to report in to the Police that we were safe and explain confidentially what had happened.

It turned out, as we found out later, the minute Dad had arrived home that Friday night and discovered we had gone he went straight out and called at every person's house that he thought we might have gone to. And just like a Miss Marple case, Mum had made a critical mistake; before leaving Ballydunn that night Mum had asked David to stop the car at one of her friend's houses to throw some work keys through the letter box. Little did we know that as Mum left her friend looked out the window at the noise of the letter box clinking and saw Mum get into a red and black car. Well, later that night when Dad had gone on a desperate rampage calling with anyone closely related to us to see if they were hiding us or knew anything about our whereabouts, he called to this house. Unaware of what mystery she was solving for my Dad, she told him what she saw and that was it! Dad knew instantly what had happened and I can only imagine the rage which ensued. He knew we had gone off with David. I can honestly say that, if Dad had found us that night, I really think he would have killed us all.

Armed with this knowledge, Dad found my brother Jack to let him know what had happened. Now the only thing Dad knew about David for certain was where his parents lived because, if you remember, Dad used to work with all of them. So late that Friday night, in raging form, Dad and Jack got a taxi the whole sixty miles to David's parents' house outside Belfast.

Of course, Mum and I didn't know any of this at the time; or rather I didn't. I only found it all out a while later. Dad and Jack arrived at their house and demanded to know where we were. I guess they would have been terrified when they arrived on their doorstep. Thankfully David's parents were able to settle them and say they didn't exactly know where we were hiding out and, for some reason, which surprised us all, Dad believed them and returned home with no other choice.

I am not fully aware of all what happened the next few weeks but I just knew life was very different and not in the way I had hoped. My safe house didn't feel safe and welcoming. And while I knew we couldn't go back to what had been my home I knew that is where I really wanted to be. And Christmas was nearly upon us and it didn't feel very Christmassy or special.

The next Saturday Mum and David took me out Christmas shopping. I even remember the store we went into it. And it is at this point Santa ceased to exist in my life. Nobody said anything but all of a sudden I knew. It was like everything associated with and since 7 December – I was no longer a child, or so it seemed. I literally had been forced to grow up overnight. So, standing there in that toy store with Mum asking me what I wanted for Christmas I just knew. There, another fairy tale gone! Another small piece of hope for peace and joy destroyed forever. At that point I didn't feel there was much hope left. This was not the fairy tale I had dreamed of.

Mum bought me a few things that day for me to use immediately; they weren't to keep for Christmas. You see running away that memorable night in a hurry we hadn't been able to lift everything we had planned to bring. So I had very few dolls or toys with me. I had brought a book of Hans Christian Andersen fairy tales, one of my school prizes, with me and I read the tales over and over again. In one way I wanted to immerse myself in a dream world where 'Happy Ever After' did really exist. But I also felt desperate to keep practising my reading as I hadn't been to school for weeks. So that afternoon with this immediate lack of Santa realisation I started to worry about Christmas Day itself and what would happen to us all. Would I have any presents to open? Would there be any excitement or fun? That night I sat and read one of the Christmas annuals Mum had bought me. Then, using some of the Christmas wrapping paper we had bought, I wrapped it up for me and put it under the tree. That way, I knew I had something to open on Christmas morning.

Around that time I found out that, with the news of our sudden departure and my Dad's deteriorating physical and mental state, my sister had come home to look after him. That was when somehow it was agreed Mum, David and I would go back to what I still called my home for a visit on Christmas Day. I cannot really remember the details of Christmas morning too well. Looking back I probably buried it deep inside in the hope it would feel less painful. I do recall getting a few presents but I couldn't tell you what I got exactly. However, I do remember smirking to myself when I opened the annual I had already read! As I said, the rest of the day was a bit of a mixed blur. There was no Christmas dinner or anything. I do recall travelling home to Ballydunn in David's car. Again, I am not sure precisely what time we headed off or anything about the journey except that Mum never said a word. The journey was eerily silent and I wondered if we would leave the house alive. It must have been strange for all of us, not knowing what lay ahead when we reached home and saw my dad.

One thing I do remember vividly is what happened when we got there. It was awful. David had parked the car around the corner from our house and he must have stayed there while Mum and I went in. Even walking to the house from the car felt like 'walking the plank'. I was mixed with emotions. I had missed Dad and John and felt excited to see them again. But then suddenly I remembered that these circumstances were far from normal and I dreaded going inside and what would happen.

I will never forget the scene when I opened the back door. Dad was sitting in the kitchen beside the electric fire, trembling with a whiskey in his hand. He just looked up and his eyes were red sore from crying and too much drink. My sister was acting as mediator. When I got in Dad gave me an almighty hug and cried hysterically. It's strange but I cannot exactly remember how I reacted. I think I was just numb. I was then taken into the front sitting room and I think my brother sat with me while Mum and Dad talked in the kitchen.. I don't know what my brother and I did – maybe we watched TV. I seriously cannot recall. I was listening intently for shouts or crying; I was really prepared for hearing a scream or a gunshot. That is how bad it was. That was how terrified I felt. My sister had been looking after Dad for the last week or so and had given him valium to calm him down. He had promised everyone he would not shout or raise his voice at any of us. Those must have been the conditions under which Mum agreed to go back. I think we must have stayed an hour or so but suddenly Mum said that it was time to leave. My sister came and got me and entering the kitchen I heard Dad ask Mum why she had left him and if she would please come home. He was pleading for us to stay at this stage. Mum just said that she would never come back. Mum looked stronger and more bitter towards my dad than I had ever seen her. I am not sure whether she had more strength now that she had had already fled or she had more courage because she knew David was waiting outside and she could escape to another life. But she walked out the door with her head high and never looked back.

For me it was a completely different scene. I didn't want to stay as I was scared what was about to erupt. But equally I didn't want to go back to the safe house. I felt lost and trapped. But I was quickly brought out of my indecision by my mum screaming for me to hurry on. I left home for the very last time to the sound of my dad in pieces; a truly broken man. And then strangely, Dad asked if he could walk us to the car; he knew David was waiting on us around the corner. Again my mind went into overdrive – what was he going to do. Was he going to kill David? Was he going to kill himself? Was there going to be a terrible scene in the middle of the estate on Christmas Day? I am sure all the neighbours knew by now what had been going on with us. I felt petrified.

So my sister and Dad walked Mum and I to the car and spoke briefly through the window to David; nothing more than hello, I think. It was all really surreal. I was waiting for something to kick off – half expecting my dad to attack David or one of us. But nothing. I hugged Dad goodbye which was really hard because I hadn't had the chance to say goodbye, before. You remember we had fled that night on the 7 December. I do not know which of us squeezed the tightest. It was as if we were holding on like grim death. I really thought we were both going to die with heartache. I think my sister eventually peeled my fingers off Dad and put me into the car. It was all a blur then. I think there was some calm hysteria. Then David drove off.

That was when I truly realised this was it, this was my new life! I didn't care about the fairy tale palaces or fancy food or clothes anymore, warts and all, fear and terror, I wanted to turn back home. I wanted my dad. Obviously at that point I was remembering the coffee, the *Call My Bluff* nights and the hair combing. I wasn't dwelling on the nasty memories. But it was too late anyway.

The next few weeks were really strange. Obviously I needed to go to school somewhere. I had already missed about one month. That worried me. One morning, without much warning, Mum told me we were going to visit what would probably be my new school for the remainder of Primary seven. We walked about twenty minutes down the country road until we reached what I can only describe as Northern Ireland's answer to the school in *The Little House in the Prairie*. It was called Charley Memorial. I was gobsmacked. It was a quaint, whitewashed little school with a tiny playground and outside toilets. We went into see the headmaster, Mr Scott, who was extremely welcoming, a man in about his late fifties, early sixties, with grey hair and the warmest smile. He told us a little about the school – there were only about thirty pupils in total and he taught Primary four Primary five, Primary six and Primary seven himself all in the same room. In contrast, I had come from a large primary school in Ballydunn with about sixty pupils in each year with an assembly hall, gymnasium, outside sports pitches, and a large canteen. Charley Memorial had two classrooms one of which doubled up or rather trebled as a classroom and dining room and anything else needed. It would take a lot of getting used to! So not long after that I started school and it was just OK. I made a few friends, one of which is still a close friend to this day. But I didn't really enjoy the rest of my time there. It was all too new. And I felt very self-conscious of what the other kids knew of my background. Thankfully I only had to go there for about six months until my primary school days were over!

Before I left Millfield Primary School I had already sat my exam (called the '11-plus' exam in those days in Northern Ireland) to determine whether I had passed to apply for a grammar school or whether I had to settle for a secondary school. Now, having moved to Clough, I had to consider which grammar and secondary schools interested me, as I was now far away from my original choices of school in Ballydunn. So Mr Scott stepped in with his expert advice and in the end, with my high score in the 11 plus, I applied and was accepted into Victoria College, Belfast. Quite an achievement apparently – a very elite grammar school in a posh part of Belfast, for young ladies!

We were still living in the safe house that we had moved to that cold, dark December night a few months ago. Not much had changed since the first night I arrived. It just looked a bit different, probably because I was seeing it from a different perspective. Yet it was my new home now – there was a bit more furniture in it now and it was a bit more organized, as the night we had arrived there random pieces of furniture were just piled up in the middle of the kitchen! I had been sleeping in the same bed as my mum since we got there. In fact I had spent a lot of time in bed trying to keep my reading up while I was missing school as I didn't want to fall behind. So I read over and over again my fairy tales; I had managed to salvage some of my books before we fled.

One night David came into our bedroom late at night and sat on the floor beside Mum and started whispering and then crying, I think. I had been sleeping and I sort of awoke to the noise but I pretended I was asleep – I was good at that, well I'd had years of experience. I tried to hear what was going on. I think the gist of it was Mum must have told him that we were going to go back to Dad because of me but he begged her not to leave. I was never aware of any conversations to that effect before that night and certainly none since. We weren't going anywhere!

Outside there was a small front garden. Directly out the back door was a right of way where the other neighbours would walk or drive up and own. Then there was a garage and a long back garden that led to the country fields.

I hated the open right of way bit outside the back door, hated it. It meant if we wanted to walk out the back door to go anywhere it was highly likely that the other neighbours would see you. This wasn't necessarily such an awful thing except if you were me. When we arrived there I could imagine all the neighbours huddled together trying to work out who we were and the family dynamics – David was a lot younger than Mum; in fact, he was younger than my two eldest brothers! So to others David could have looked like Mum's son rather than her partner. So for me, heading out the back of the house was filled with panic and I avoided it like the plague.

Clough comprised of a few rows of similar terraced houses. The neighbours had all been there for years, generation after generation and some were interrelated.

There weren't many new additions to the neighbourhood so I guessed we would feature as a common talking point for quite some time! I eventually got to like Clough. I made a few friends, of which you will read later on.

After that horrible Christmas night my contact with my dad for the next year or so was very irregular and always upsetting for us both. I think the next time I saw him he came up by train to a town near Clough with Jack and we all a met in a pub – of course, where else? It was Mum, Dad, Jack, David and I – all very awkward. Anyway, my mum had filed for divorce and so the main conversation was the court case. I think that was the reason they came up. Jack took me out to walk around while they talked a bit, so I didn't hear too much. But at parting time, it was rather distressing; Dad clinging to me and us both crying sore.

The next few months I later found out that Mum and Dad had gone to court – I never knew at the time because I was at school. But at some point Mum did tell me that the case had not gone as planned and the divorce was not granted. It seems when Mum spoke open and honestly about their relationship and my Dad's mental and physical abuse Dad lied – even on oath in the witness stand. He said she was making it all up because she was having an affair. So, it ended with Mum not being granted the divorce and instead Dad being given access to see me every other Saturday when Mum would have to take me by train to Ballydunn to see him. So that is what happened. They never ever got that divorce.

Initially I looked forward to seeing Dad at the weekends. Again, I was clinging to the good memories, albeit they were few. But in the end he was my dad and I missed him. Mum and I would go by train to Ballydunn every other Saturday morning. The plan was Dad would meet me off the train, take me somewhere and have me back for the teatime train home again. But it didn't go as smoothly as intended. He would meet me at the train station and we would end up in one of his local pubs, surrounded by his old drunken cronies. He would then usually take me to the sweet shop and the days he was feeling flush he would just buy me loads of sweets as if that was all I needed or wanted. I really started getting upset by it all – inwardly of course, I didn't say anything to anyone. I just wished we could have done something different. By that stage the pub was symbolic to me of all the troubled nights I had tried to put to the back of my mind. Pubs and excessive drinking reminded me of Dad's aggressive nature.

Most Saturdays, he was usually quite calm and pleasant with me during the visits but horrid memories would flood in every so often. I just wanted to have quality time with him, perhaps go to the park or visit his mum and dad, my grandparents. I hadn't seen them since we left, in fact I never ever saw them again! They both passed away shortly after that. No, we never did anything different. Then, when it was time to go home – well, what can I say? I dreaded the homeward journey. I sometimes tried to persuade Dad to leave me down the street and I would walk the last bit to the train station on my own. But of course that never happened. Dad would leave me to the train station as promised and Mum would be there waiting for me. But instead of Dad leaving after saying goodbye he would wait until the train arrived and wait for us to board. Then the scene came, he would then get on the train after us and start getting visibly upset; crying and begging us to get off the train and come home for good. It was awful. I was really upset and embarrassed. Everyone was looking at us. Sometimes he stayed on the train for a few stops and eventually got off miles away. Then I would worry how he would get home as he was so far away and probably didn't have much money left. I ended up dreading those visits. I felt deep down I was falling apart.

As time went by the visits got less and less and they gradually fizzled out. I don't ever remember why or if someone said anything or if something particular had happened. But I don't think Dad complained. He had met another woman and had started a new life with her – ironically she was also called Jill, just like my mum! He started living with her in Portlouth just around the corner from his parents' house. She was a nice lady, a widow, with two grown-up sons in America. I suppose they were company for each other; they were both quite clever – they enjoyed doing the crosswords together and going to quizzes. They often went out to the British Legion and had a wee dance. A few times he went with her to the States to visit her sons. He helped her around the house and she benefitted from having a man around to do those nasty jobs only men want and can do. Plus, I must admit I felt relieved he had someone else; someone to care for him and keep him company. I used to worry about him so much. Even though I was young and I knew he had done wrong, he was still my dad and I loved him.

I didn't see Dad much after that for quite some time. There was the random phone call or card but no real commitment or regular arrangements for contact like there had been. My thoughts and feelings about life were starting to become concerning but I was scared to say anything to anyone. I felt completely alone.

AND SO IT BEGAN

In September 1980 it was time to start Victoria College. I was quite anxious but excited at the same time. I didn't know anybody really. The only time I had been to visit the school was on one of the open days in June and David had dropped Mum and I off at one of the main entrances. But on the first morning Mum put me on the bus in Clough on my own. I was terrified. I didn't know which bus stop to get off. I didn't know Belfast at all. So I asked someone and got off where they said. As I turned around the corner I saw crowds of girls in Victoria uniforms so I just followed them. I hadn't recognised where I was; it turned out that I was on a completely different road and going in a different entrance to the school than the Open Day.

Let me start by telling you I loved Victoria College. I got a great education there and met loads of really good friends. The fact that it was an all-girls' school did not bother me at all. In fact I quite enjoyed the fact that there was no distraction from boys, especially as the years passed by. I think, from hearing about girls from other mixed schools, the presence of boys made the girls bitchier and your focus on school slightly distorted at times! Victoria was quite posh and had a reputation of being a grammar school for young ladies! Sometimes I liked that; sometimes I didn't! We had to change into indoor brown sandals once in school and our uniform was very prim and proper. We studied less common subjects such as Latin and Greek, not many grammar schools in Northern Ireland did that.

While I liked going to Victoria, I learnt very quickly that I did not exactly fit in with the majority of the other girls. There were a few types of girls who went to Victoria. The first group were the boarders and there were three types of boarders; some girls boarded from various parts of the globe such as China, Australia or Africa whose parents either worked away from home a lot and wanted their daughters to have a stable education or the family lived abroad and had heard of the excellent reputation of Victoria and wanted to send their daughter to become a young lady! Then there were the boarders who lived in Northern Ireland outside of Belfast but whose parents thought the daily commute would be too demanding; and finally there were those girls who had not obtained sufficient grades to get into Victoria and so the only way was with money via boarding – most of them went home at weekends. I always felt sorry for the boarders who had to stay at school as such week in week out, it must have been awful. There was this one girl – from China – she could hardly speak any English and we couldn't even pronounce her name so we called her Charlotte Chang – and another girl who we named Winnie Wong! We sat many a lunchtime trying to teach them English to get through the classes – my heart really went out to them! The boarders always stayed around each other and didn't really bother too much with non-boarders. I suppose they lived with each other 24/7 basically so they were like one big family. And then... there were the rich girls. Now do not get me wrong they were not all rich bitches, far from it really, the majority of them were really nice and some became really close friends of mine – in fact most of them didn't really appreciate how well-off they actually were. They mostly lived in and around the school in the most expensive residential parts of Belfast. Listening to their daily lives was like reading a story in Hello magazine! One friend in particular mentioned Cliff Richard was staying with them for a few nights, as if it was any normal friend popping round for tea!

The well-off girls were usually dropped off to school in their parents' fancy sports cars. Their family lives too sounded so perfect, going on holidays and outings with their perfect parents and they spoke of proper family meals and food I had never even heard of. But all in all they were really innocent girls. Most of them had attended Victoria's preparatory school and so they had been enrolled to go to Victoria from birth, really. They all knew one another really well. But as I say they were lovely.

And finally, there was the third small group of girls who went to Victoria with whom I fitted right in – we were the working-class lot! I am not sure if it bothered the others as much as me. We didn't really say too much in that way. However, sometimes I felt really insecure. Because not only was I in what I considered the lowest group – class-speaking – I felt I was the lowest of the low. My family circumstances were unspeakable and so I adopted a pretend life. I didn't want anyone knowing my real life and from where I had come. What was I to say? Oh yes, Mum and I fled in the middle of the night when I was ten from my abusive, alcoholic father, not telling anyone, to a safe house, we don't have very much money, my mum works at night as a waitress to earn a few pounds to send me to this school and now my mum's partner happens to be my dad's former friend, a few years younger than my two eldest brothers… Yip, that would have been great classroom gossip – I would really have been everyone's best friend then!

So I pretended my life was different; I made up a family and I made up where I lived. One day in the depths of winter, one of my friend's parents offered me a lift home from school as they were driving my direction. I was scared to say no and couldn't think of a reasonable excuse. So, what did I do? Knowing I couldn't let them see where I really lived I got them to leave me off at a house down the road which I always thought looked lovely. I didn't want my friends knowing the real me and so I made loads of stuff up. Looking back, I keep asking myself why. Firstly, I think I was desperate to be accepted as part of the gang, I tried to be someone I thought others would want to be with. I was really continuing my role as a people-pleaser, being compliant with everyone at all times. Secondly, I think, I wanted to pretend and convince myself my life was different. I didn't like who I was and from where I had come. I felt ashamed and dirty – so I went to extreme measures to hide the real me. I couldn't let others in. I just couldn't. What if they didn't like the real me?

My first year in Victoria was quite tough, from the academic point of view – many of the subjects were really new to me and I never had anyone at home to help me. David never really said too much to me; he was a quiet man and I think he was starting to wonder what he had let himself in for. By this time my brother John had moved in with us too. I remember reality starting to hit him because one night John and I were arguing over what we would watch on TV in the sitting room. In those days there was only one television in the house, well in our house anyway – and suddenly like an exploding volcano David just literally erupted – telling us to keep quiet, to give him peace and to remember we were in his house.

I really felt alone. I had no one I could turn to for help with schoolwork or anything for that matter. And as for my mum, bless her, I definitely didn't dream of asking Mum for help. As I mentioned before, academia was not her strong point, so it was all down to me. Mum never had to ask me to do my homework; she saw that I worked hard. She never really got involved in the school stuff. She wouldn't have known if I had done everything or not. If Dad had been around I would have asked him for help; but he wasn't. So I had to do it all myself. I quickly became my own dictator; a martyr to myself as well as others. I felt quite under pressure that first year in Victoria, but I tried my best.

The next problem came when the exams were approaching. I didn't really know how to revise and, as many of you reading this will know, revision is an art, it is a skill all on its own, a skill that requires a student, young or old, to know how to plan, prioritise and actually discover the best way to study and learn. Most of the other schoolgirls had been taught this skill all the way through Victoria preparatory school so they were already streets ahead of the rest of us. I had to teach myself everything, not only the subject matter but the discipline required to study. So here I was struggling in the first year. To be honest I didn't really revise because I didn't know how to. Therefore, I wasn't properly prepared for my first year exams in Victoria. So not surprisingly my results could have been much better. They were all right, don't get me wrong, but not up to the extremely high standards and expectations I was starting to set myself. I was fine when it came to Maths; I had always been quite a natural mathematician. However, when it came to things like Chemistry and Physics I was lost! I hated science which made the study of it even harder. It is very hard to learn anything if you are not interested in the subject matter. Consequently, following the first set of exam results I went through a massive phase of dissatisfaction with myself. Why had I performed so badly? For the first time in my life I was not top of the class. I had been top of everything all the way through primary school. I had achieved a super result in the transfer test and now I had fallen to average. I found it hard to cope with the emotions the feelings of failure instilled in me. And of course I didn't dare say to anyone because I was too embarrassed. Not only was I leading a pretend life in school but at home too; with the closest family members I was not being totally truthful either – I was terrified of being seen as a failure! The psychological battle inside me was beginning and I didn't even know!

In light of my first year exam results, I was put into the middle class for second year. I was really disappointed in myself. I felt like a failure. No one else seemed to care; I don't recall anything ever being said at home and at that time I don't recall me being in direct contact with my sister and brothers too much. Mum would have spoken to them but, to be honest, my academic abilities wouldn't have featured too much in her conversations. No, it was only me beating myself up – I had become my own punitive parent. I was showing the initial signs of a mental illness. I swore that my poor performance would never happen again. I had to study more and get into the top class. And guess what, I did. I was in the top class ever since – but at a price!

Up until then I think I ate like any normal working-class kid, with your staple of mashed potatoes almost every night, with bacon or mince, followed by puddings and the usual junk; sweets, crisps and chocolate. Haute cuisine or à la carte certainly didn't feature. There were certainly no pasta or salad dishes to talk about. I took packed lunches to Victoria which involved a few sandwiches, crisps and some juice. But while I was in second and third year in school a few different things happened which probably triggered the fatal anorexia nervosa switch.

As I mentioned before, contact at this stage with my brothers and my sister was quite limited. There was no such thing as Skype, Facebook or Instagram. So you largely relied on actually meeting up. Sometimes when Mum and I went to Ballydunn to see my Granny O'Hara, Mum's mum, or other aunts, uncles or cousins would have arranged to be there too so we could see them all at the same time. Sometimes my brother Jack met us there. It got quite boring just listening to the adults chat and they often wanted me out of the way anyway so Mum could tell them all that was going on. Then one day, I remember it well, a few of my cousins were there and we went out to my granny and grandad's small backyard to play ball. Then, totally out of the blue – one of them called me fatso! I was shocked and deeply embarrassed. No one else said anything so I am not sure if they thought the same or hadn't really heard what had been said. I composed myself and continued to play as if nothing had happened. But something had happened. Something highly significant. Little did I know then how one word would impact the rest of my life. I know they were only having fun but I still do not know why they said it... we will never know; even in my low opinion of myself I do not honestly think I was getting fat... Now while I was aware of what they had said it didn't have any immediate direct impact on me or my behaviour, but looking back I do think it was Strike 1.

The next significant event came when there was a twenty-four hour sponsored fast organised in school to raise funds for charity. It was to take place from six p.m. Friday night until six p.m. Saturday night so as not to interfere with the school day. So I volunteered, got a few sponsors and fasted. I found the fasting fine, it didn't really challenge me too much and so when 6 p.m. arrived I felt so proud of myself. I had achieved something for myself and raised money to help others. Almost instantly I decided I would continue to fast until the next day! Strike 2! Let battle commence. Anorexia was already taking hold and I didn't know!

The next major incident involved one of my mum's puddings. I can picture it vividly: this one night Mum made me a big bowl of sticky strawberry jam sponge pudding, covered in fresh cream on one side and hot custard on the other. Now I ate it and at the time thought it was great. However, a few hours later it was a different story – I was so ill, I vomited for days. It got so bad I was vomiting green bile; there was nothing left in my stomach. It took ages for me to get back on my feet, but what I then realised was that I had lost quite a few pounds; and it felt amazing! Strike 3!

Soon afterwards came another major turning point; I was about fifteen by this stage and my best friend Janet and I used to hang around with each other all the time outside of school. You see, Janet went to the local high school, poles apart from Victoria. In fact most of Clough went to Dunmurry High. So Janet and I tried to see each other as much as we could at evenings, during the weekend and at holiday times. It was at Dunmurry, which was a mixed school, that she met her first boyfriend Nigel. He was two years above Janet in school so approximately two years older than us. I heard lots about him and, of course, as young teenage girls do, she told me everything about their romance. It all sounded so exciting and fun to me. I was still so innocent and obviously, going to Victoria, I didn't encounter the daily flirting which seemed to go on in mixed schools just like another part of the curriculum. As time went by Nigel used to come up to Janet's house, quite a walk away for him but, hey, that was young love for you! So I got to meet him a few times and, I cannot deny, he was quite nice, very well dressed for such a young guy. He followed the Mods' dress style – and for those readers who are not familiar with that era, that involved sharp suits, small collared shirts, ties and pointy, well-polished shoes. Just the type of perfectly manicured first boyfriend you are happy to introduce to your parents! He was from a fairly well-off family background too which is always another bonus! Then this one night, I remember it vividly – 21 March 1984, is my memory good or what? Yip, sadly too good, as you will have learnt – I had just called at Janet's for a catch-up when her front door knocked. It was Nigel and one of his friends, Simon. Now, something I could never understand, as Janet was from quite a strict, religious family, was how she was allowed to have Nigel into her front room to visit. I never could understand that, to be honest; but she was. Her parents were obviously very naive or very trusting of their daughter – misplaced on the odd occasion I must add! Anyway, on this night, Janet invited both Nigel and Simon in. You see where this is going?

So we all got talking and of course, after a short while, Janet and Nigel got quite close and that left Simon and I alone. We chatted, got to know each other and then it all started. My first real boyfriend! The next few days were quite exciting. Again, may I remind you, no mobile phones in those days so instant and constant communication using texting, Facebook, Instagram was not an option. We had to settle for good old landline calls to the house, whenever we were allowed, but mainly it was down to meeting up at the weekends. The first few weeks, I couldn't wait for Janet to call over after school and report back stories and messages from Simon. She would tell me how in love he seemed. We would all meet up at weekends; Janet and I would normally walk the few miles to Dunmurry and just hang around. It was all very innocent. The weeks and months flew by and I can honestly say I thought I had fallen in love. It was such a great feeling. At Victoria I was probably one of the few girls to have a boyfriend and my friends loved to hear about my relationship with Simon. It was again probably typical of the posh/working class divide I found myself in at school.

I didn't dare bring Simon into my house, the closest he got to speaking to Mum or David was calling to my door or ringing the house phone if they happened to answer. And the phone calls became another issue over time. Calls were costly in those days so often I was not allowed to use the phone; days could have passed without us even talking to each other. Sometimes Simon resorted to writing me letters – yes, remember pen and paper? I can imagine many a raised eyebrow from some of you. He was such a romantic and the letters he wrote could have been straight out of a Danielle Steele novel; they would have brought tears to a stone! I used to take them to school and my friends were stunned that someone of our age could profess their love in such an innocent way. He was always buying me wee gifts, sending me records (CDs did not exist yet!) and carrying out a number of romantic gestures. He even used to ring the school and say he was my brother and there was an emergency at home and I would have to ring him back immediately. That happened a few times and eventually the secretaries caught on! Then for our six-month anniversary he saved up and bought me the most gorgeous little ring! I was head over heels, I had fallen hook, line and sinker – we both had. And as with anyone's first love, I couldn't imagine or dare to think of life without him. I really felt loved and an inner happiness that I had never experienced before.

Now, a couple of things I forgot to mention, which I need to tell you now to set the context. First was the fact that by now, Mum had got me a part-time job in the Country Inn, where she worked. Looking back, I was far too young to be out working in a pub a few nights a week especially coming up to my exam years. However, again it was indicative of how little my mum really understood my education. She just thought that I could earn a few pounds for myself as money was getting in greater demand as I was getting older. And secondly, it was another fine example of t my working-background. I am sure some of my school friends' parents frowned on the fact that I worked in a pub, I could tell. In fact one of my best school friend's parents forbade me from going to their house and told me I was not good enough to befriend their daughter. That hurt, I really took that to heart. From very early on, as you have read, I tried to please everyone, I needed desperately for everyone to like me. That is how insecure and vulnerable I felt. But to most of my class apparently I was rather cool, working in a pub, boyfriend in tow – quite the rebel and odd one out for a young lady at Victoria!

The other thing I need to mention is my next door neighbour. Why would that be significant, I hear you wonder? Well it is, read on. Our next door neighbours were the McCandlesses: mum, dad and three sons. The eldest two were in their late teens at that time and had become good friends with my brother John. They were all into motorbikes and would have gone out to the pub for a few drinks or a game of snooker or pool. Innocent enough stuff. The youngest of the three was called Charlie; he was in the same year as Nigel and Simon at Dunmurry so they all knew each other. So he too was about two years older than me. Since I went to live in Clough I always thought he looked really attractive with short, jet-black hair, and big brown eyes and the longest eyelashes I have ever seen on a guy and quite swarthy skin. He would often run about in jeans and a black leather jacket. In fact I knew from Janet and others that he was a real stud at Dunmurry High School. But over the years Charlie and I had become friends and we used to chat a lot. In fact at night when I was up in my bedroom, if he passed by and saw my light on he would often throw a stone at my window and, if I heard it, I would open the window and we would chat for ages. It was like a scene from *Romeo and Juliet*! To be honest I did fancy him but guessed he was way out of my league. Other times if he passed by our front sitting room window and see me sitting doing homework he would wave for me to go to the door and, again, we would chat away for hours. I knew he went out with other girls so I never ever thought I had a hope. My self-esteem had always been quite low; I thought I was quite ugly and certainly had no supermodel figure. He also used to tease me about being a lady and thought I was a snob because I went to Victoria.

So when I started dating Simon, Charlie seemed very surprised; I began to detect a little jealousy. I thought it couldn't be; he wasn't interested in me. But lo and behold, as time went on there definitely was a spark between us. We all used to hang about the street in Clough, there was quite a crowd of us. It was all good craic as we say here in Northern Ireland and we would chat, play rounders or some other game. We were all in our young/middle teens and it was all good, innocent banter. There was no worry of excessive drinking, drugs or legal highs back then, thank goodness. I found growing up bad enough. And as time went on, Charlie and I definitely became closer friends. Then Charlie started coming to the Country Inn some nights when I was working and so we would strike up more conversations. He would often come in with other girls usually way older than him. I definitely never thought anything would come of him and me, besides I was going out with Simon anyway at that stage.

As I was now working in the bar a few nights a week and I had to study for my forthcoming O levels (as they were then – known as GCSEs nowadays) my time with Simon became rather limited. We would still chat on the phone as much as we could but we usually were only able to meet up maybe once a week, or even once every two weeks.

I quite resented having to work; I was exhausted and I really needed to be at home to study. The nights I worked meant I really had no time for homework or revision at all. By the time I got home from school it was near five and I had to get tea, sorted for school the next day, changed into my work uniform and be at the pub for around seven. I was then on my feet the whole night and some nights I wouldn't get home to after midnight. I had to be up again before seven to get the bus to school in Belfast. On a couple of occasions I actually fell asleep in class. This was just no good. I felt I was being pulled in every direction. I felt severely under pressure to be good at everything: do well at school and be the perfect student; spend time with Simon and be the model girlfriend; and keep my job and earn some money to be the obedient daughter. I felt I was constantly trying to make time to do everything and please everybody and was scared to complain to anyone or let the real truth out! It wasn't easy! It was only a matter of time before something was going to give. I was setting myself up for failure; the pressure I was putting myself under was extremely stressful – I was my own strict parent!

So the following May, in the lead-up to my important exams Simon and I were only able to see each other one weekend night every two weeks. Between working in the pub and studying that was all I could fit in but Simon seemed to understand and we knew it was only for a few weeks until the exams were over. Then one Friday night when I was actually supposed to be meeting Simon he rang to say he had to go to a wake; a friend's grandfather had died the day before. While obviously disappointed I understood and said I would study instead and we could see each other the following Friday instead. I never thought any more of it.

However, the following night I was working in the Country Inn and one of the barmen said he thought he had seen my beloved the previous night. I said he must have been mistaken as Simon was at a wake. A few nights later, I was sitting doing homework by the window as usual and Charlie passed by outside and pointed for me to go to the front door. So I did; we chatted for a while; just general stuff. He then asked me what happened to Simon and me. I was quite confused and said I didn't understand what he was talking about. Charlie said he too had been in the Country Inn the previous Friday night and bumped into Simon with a crowd of guys and girls. I was stunned. I just didn't know what to say. I felt gutted. I felt betrayed and abandoned. Simon had lied to me. Instead of him being at a wake he had gone out with friends and appeared quite cozy with some other girl. But not just out anywhere, to my place of work, where staff and customers knew me and him. What was he playing at? He hadn't loved me after all. Why could nobody really love me? What had I done wrong? Why had I failed in keeping him?

So the rest of the evening was over as far as schoolwork was concerned. I decided to go outside with the Clough gang. Charlie came over to comfort me and we went over what had happened again. So he accompanied me to the red phone box on the corner of the street. Yes imagine having to find a local phone box and literally insert coins before you could ring someone – how old do I feel? Anyway, with some strangely instant strength and determination I rang Simon. I confronted the subject and before he could even answer, I said it was over and put the phone down – that was 15 May 1985. Looking back, I can see Simon was one of the few males in my life who had been nothing but good to me; he had given me all the attention, love and security I had never had but had so desperately needed. He had made me genuinely happy until he betrayed and hurt me… and that was it…

The following days were a massive turning point in my life. I felt different. I felt low. I felt rejected. I felt abandoned by the only person I thought truly loved me and now he had hurt me, just like everyone else. What was wrong with me? Could I ever trust anyone ever again? So I became determined that Simon would regret what he had done to me. I was obviously not good enough for him. So what could I do? I know, I would have to change the way I looked. Almost immediately, my eating habits started to change…

MY SECRET FRIEND

I executed my plan immediately. I started exercising more than usual. I would make up dance routines to the sounds in the charts and I would watch myself in the mirror in my bedroom or in the sitting room if no one else was in the house. I became more aware of what I ate. Now, do not get me wrong, there was no immediate starvation or extreme behaviour; it was more a gradual change. I would swap my mum's heavy, stodgy dinners for salads every night. My salads became a work of art. Everything was all intricately laid out on the plate in colourful patterns. I began skipping breakfast and had black coffee instead. At school I exchanged my previous sandwiches and chocolate with fruit or celery or cucumber – definitely a healthy bite of some description. And of course the weight slowly began to fall off. And that was it – I had made a new friend – it was like I was having a secret affair with someone who truly understood me, who knew how to make me happy, knew the inner me and promised never to hurt me! How could I refuse such a relationship?

As time went by, the more people commented on my weight loss the happier I felt. I had achieved something, I felt more in control than I ever did. I was changing the way I looked; I was hoping the thinner I was the more attractive I would be. Simon and anyone else who had ever doubted me or looked down on me would see what I could really look like. They would regret how they had hurt me.

I was about sixteen at this stage; still working in the Country Inn, still studying hard for my exams, and still trying to juggle all the balls. In fact I was in fourth year and was going to sit my Maths and English O levels a year early! Charlie and I had started dating and I genuinely thought I was falling in love again. I still harboured feelings for Simon but they were different now. I was determined to make him regret how he had betrayed me. I would make him want me back. But I would never give in. Never. That determination got stronger and with it so did the power of my anorexia. Or my secret friend as I called her! I could never let go of what I had found now. No one would ever take my new friend away. We had become inseparable. I felt as long as I had her I would be fine. She was all I needed. I just had to keep her happy and do what she said!

My daily routines had changed. They had become more demanding, I was punishing myself and I didn't realise it. I seemed to be working all the time either at school, studying at home or in the pub. I was also desperately trying to fit in time for Charlie. Deep down I was now scared of losing him too. I was eating less and less and even the girls in school started to comment. I was ecstatic with the effect of my grueling new lifestyle. I was winning; I was good at this, and I wasn't hurting anyone! By this stage my periods had become extremely irregular, practically non-existent. But I didn't care, I knew I wasn't pregnant. I felt more and more in control. I wasn't eating anything at all which could have been construed as the slightest bit unhealthy – so no big dinners, no potatoes or chips, no chocolate, sweets, crisps. Nothing like that! From then on, it was really only salads, fruit, All-Bran and to drink, water or black coffee or tea. It never really varied. Every mealtime became an intricate ritual. I had to eat the same thing, at the same time and preferably on my own which was extremely difficult. I was beginning to feel really guilty about being seen eating, as if I was unworthy or didn't need or deserve to eat.

My secret friend had taken over. My secret life was really the one in full control, I was like a puppet doing as I was told. She literally pulled all the strings! In my head she told me what I could and could not eat. She told me when I should exercise and when I could rest, which wasn't often. But stupidly or naively, whichever way you look at it, I felt I was in control. I had been completely brainwashed.

Things continued like this for a good few months and then something major happened.

Now I have to set the scene. I was still working a few nights a week in the pub, still in a relationship with Charlie, and still trying to keep everyone happy. One thing I need to tell you is that, behind my back, and to my total surprise, Charlie had got a part-time job in the Ulster Defence Regiment (UDR)! Now for those of you who do not know what the UDR was, let me explain. It was the army in Northern Ireland. And particularly, during the Troubles here, it was one of the most dangerous jobs to be in. Your life was really at risk. Many UDR soldiers were killed, seriously injured and traumatised by things they had witnessed and things they had to do in their job. I was horrified that he had gone and joined particularly without even mentioning it to me. I was immediately worried that something awful was going to happen to him and I was going to lose him. He was only eighteen at the time and still living in some boyish fantasy that he could save the world and make a difference. To be honest it was really about earning a few extra pounds. He had a day job as a carpet-fitter but it didn't pay much and the outlook was bleak. So he obviously thought he would get a part-time job too. I don't know why he couldn't have just got a few extra hours in a shop or bar like most people. No, instead he had to join the UDR.

But on top of that he had betrayed me; he had kept it all a secret from me. All that time, thinking about it, applying for it, going for the interview and getting the job and he didn't tell me any of it. I was really hurt. Worst of all was how I found out. I was getting ready to go to work one night when his mum came in, as she often did for a wee blether and cup of tea with my mum – remember we were all neighbours – and asked me what I thought about Charlie getting into the UDR. By my face she at once realised I hadn't known anything. I covered up my horror and went off to work as usual. Charlie was at home getting a shower and his mum must have gone straight in and told him what she had said to me. Thank goodness it was Friday night and I was really hectic in the Country Inn. The shock of the news hung in my head but I got through the night busy with work. One of the other waitresses gave me a lift home to the end of my street and I walked the small distance towards our house. It was after midnight by this stage and there, sitting on the wall waiting for me was Charlie. He quickly tried to explain that he hadn't wanted to worry me and didn't really think he was going to get accepted into the UDR anyway. He said he was going to tell me that night anyway and was furious with his mum for telling me. Apparently she knew I hadn't known – how nasty was that! Seeing his genuine worry about what I thought and felt, fearing we were over my anger and hurt crumbled and we hugged and cried. That was the first night of many I shed a tear during his years in the UDR.

Anyway, back to the story…

So, as I was starting to tell you, something significant happened that June. David had been working away in England with his brothers for a few months off and on. So it had been Mum and I mainly in the house. This one Wednesday afternoon I had returned home from school, full of the joys as the exams were over and school was nearly at an end, meaning no homework or studying to do. Charlie was out UDR training and Mum was working in the Country Inn that night. I had made plans earlier that day to go and see a friend, Katie, from my primary school. I hadn't seen her in ages and we were going to have a wee tea party. Mum headed off to work and after about eight I headed out too, taking my house keys with me. Mum and Charlie would both be home about eleven. My friend lived a mile or so down the road so I just walked as it was a nice, bright summer evening. I was full of the joys of spring.

I called at Katie's front door but there was no answer. That was strange, I thought. I looked around the corner of the house and I saw her dad's car so at least he must have been in the house. So I walked around to the back door; same thing! Now I did this a few times, feeling more and more confused. Katie had told me to call for her. Then, as I was walking away from the front door for about the fifth time and about half an hour later, I could see through the glass panel in the door her dad inside with a towel around him. Ooops, I didn't know what to do then. So I timidly went to the front door again and I was about to knock the door when he opened it very slowly, told me to come in but, turning his back to me, walked away.

I innocently and very shyly said, "Oh sorry for troubling you. You mustn't have heard me, Katie told me to call."

Without even turning around, he said, "Nope, I ignored you on purpose."

I can still hear those words to this day. I think I just stopped in my tracks. At that he shouted "Come in here now!"

I couldn't quite believe what he had said and was frightened by his raised voice. He continued to walk away from me and then he went into the front sitting room, very calmly, sat in one of the armchairs with his towel still around his waist, slowly lit up a cigarette, blew a small ring of smoke into the air and repeated, just staring into space, "I ignored you on purpose."

By this time I was propping myself up against the door of the sitting room. I wanted to just run but I just stood there completely numb. I just couldn't move. I was hoping Katie would appear and it would all be a big joke! But she didn't. Nobody did. It was just her dad and me. I think I mumbled a few words in shock like, "but why?" and he replied with an all too familiar vicious tirade of abuse at me. To sum it up, he said that if I wasn't good enough for his daughter. I could just f*** away off to my snobby Victoria friends. That he didn't want me near his daughter or in his house, I didn't deserve to eat his food, nor waste his electricity. He just continued to shout the same thing over and over again.

He shouted at me asking, who did I think I was getting on like that? He called me a selfish, snobby bitch and said he didn't want me near his family or in his house.

He kept telling me just to f*** off and get out. I remember being instantly terrified, I couldn't believe what I was hearing or seeing. It had come so out of the blue. He had always been such a lovely man; he sounded like a great dad, from all the stories Katie told. What had I done wrong? Why me? He was like a Jekyll and Hyde. I felt the tears streaming down my face. I was too scared to even cry and make a sound. But I was sobbing my heart out inside. I was feeling so many different things. I was shocked. I was hurt. I was scared. I felt lost. I was all alone in the house with him and then I just ran... all the way home.

It was still only about nine thirty and Mum wasn't due in for another while. I just drifted into the kitchen and sat on the floor in the dark. I sobbed quietly into myself, burying my head into my arms wrapped around my legs so as to try to muffle any sound. I just sat and waited for Mum to come home. I sat there all alone and terrified for hours. I felt so relieved to see her when she came in through the front door. She walked into the kitchen, turned on the light and jumped when she saw me in such a clearly visible state on the floor. I must have looked a real mess by that stage. It was near midnight by now and I must have crying sore for nearly three hours! She was equally as shocked to see me there and when I explained what had happened, I saw the genuine horror in her face. She spent the next hour or so trying to ring Katie's house, but there was no answer.

I think to begin with she couldn't really fathom that Katie's dad had just turned on me like that. I eventually just said I didn't want her to do anything about it and it would be best if we just left it. I was too ashamed for anyone else to find out. After a while Mum begged me to come up to bed, but I refused. I was terrified to move. I sat there on the kitchen floor for what seemed like ages. I eventually crept up to my bedroom at about three or four and lay on my bed in my clothes, in complete darkness, sobbing. I didn't sleep. I watched the clock, every minute.

When it got near six in the morning I got ready for school really quietly so as not to wake Mum. I crept into the bathroom, tried to wash the tear-stained face, grabbed my schoolbag and blazer and tiptoed out the back door. I was really early for my school bus but I decided I would rather be outside in the air waiting than inside the house not knowing what the morning would bring. Eventually the hours passed, the school bus arrived and I was on my way to school. I don't think I ever felt as glad to be going to school. However, the shock and horror of the previous night's events hadn't left me and I spent the entire day crying in the toilets. I couldn't even fully explain what happened to my friends as I was too ashamed. I could hardly tell them the truth – what would I say? Yeah one of my primary school friend's dad verbally abused me last night practically threw me out of his house, called me a snobbish bitch and told me endlessly that I didn't deserve to eat his food or waste his electricity – in fact he told me to f*** away off! Yeah I could just picture how that would go down in Victoria College. So it was easier just to say I had fallen out with Charlie and it was a lover's tiff. My friends thought that sounded reasonable, never suspected the horror behind my lies and thankfully covered for me with my teachers. What a twenty-four hours.

I dreaded going home, I really did. I didn't want to have to worry Mum with anything else. I had to straighten myself out until I could go home and tell her convincingly it was all fine and it had been a big misunderstanding. I decided not to catch the normal bus and instead hung around school for another while and go home later. I was terrified of reaching the house. Mum was standing in the kitchen when I very cautiously walked through the back door. I said I was fine and that was it. Mum looked relieved. She never really mentioned anything else and we went along our way. But it was all different from then; for me anyway. Katie's dad's voice rang in my head. I thought of all he had said, the critical, hateful words. But I tried to hide the feelings and get on with my life. I never went near Katie's house after that. Apparently, they moved far away a few months later. I never heard from her again but I think her parents divorced due to some major issues. I wasn't surprised. Her dad had been really scary.

After that horrible night I was extremely aware of everything I did and everything I said. I was conscious of each step I took, every single noise I made, every bite of food I ate and I wouldn't use electricity when Mum and David were around. The horrible, critical words kept going through my head, "I didn't deserve anything and I was a waste of space". I couldn't escape it, it was like a broken record… it just kept going on and on. My daily routines changed; life became even more bizarre. I had to plan everything out to military detail. I had to live ahead of myself all the time. I had to wash and shower when Mum and David were out or still in bed. I never used electricity unless totally vital. I wouldn't use the hairdryer or even watch TV when there were others around. And my eating and general living habits took a total nosedive. My whole being had been annihilated. I felt worthless. But I still had my friend – she became ever more present and more important to me than ever.

I truly believe this incident had a major turning point in my life, sadly for the worse. It had reiterated all the things that my illness had started to make me think about myself. That I was not important; nobody really cared about me and I deserved to be punished. My new mantra had been born.

And like all the other thousands of events in my short life, I couldn't tell anyone. I was afraid. I was ashamed. Another dirty secret to add to the long list. I would push it deep within me and pretend it never happened. Yes, that was the best way to deal with it, I thought.

I never understood why Katie's dad turned on me like that; maybe I was the punchbag he needed when his own family life was falling apart. I was an easy target on which to vent his frustration and emotions. I will never know. It has never ever been mentioned since. Not even my closest family knows about that night; well, I certainly haven't told them.

Looking back now particularly as I write this book it is hard to believe the events of that night happened, but they did. And they marred me forever.

So as I am sure you can imagine, things did not improve after that night and the anorexia nervosa took a real deep hold of me. I had sat several O levels, and done exceedingly well. I had become a real perfectionist in everything; putting extreme, unrealistic demands on myself. I was now entering into my last year at Victoria and trying to study for three A levels: French, Spanish and Latin. However, I inwardly felt torn; trying to go to school with my pretend life, study for my exams, entertain and keep Charlie as my boyfriend, be the perfect daughter in the house – it was no longer a home – and work a few nights a week to earn money so I wasn't wasting Mum's ! As I fought more to be all things to all people, the anorexia was there – my friend was there. She was my crutch, I could depend on her. But she was my secret – nobody could know. I didn't want anyone to take it or her away from me.

So I did my best at school, nobody knew anything different. Well I don't think so; comments were made on my eating habits and how much weight I was losing, and to any anorexic it was music to my ears – a compliment – I had found something I could do, excel in, be in control of! My new best friend and I became closer and closer. She was my rock – she was always there for me – day or night. She knew what I needed, I told myself! I was at her disposal and her mercy.

Looking back it was not surprising my exam results were not as glowing as I had hoped. I did well but I was distraught I hadn't achieved three As. I hated myself. I told myself I was useless – I had let everyone down; my family would be so disappointed. Before I knew it, it was time to pick universities and it all spiralled out of control. For the last while I had just been getting through each day as best as I could to make it through the exams; I hadn't thought too much about what would happen next. All my friends had talked it through with their parents and had made their options, most of them heading across the Irish Sea to Scotland and England. Earlier in the year I had visited a few universities too, but it was all a bit of a whirlwind. It hadn't really sunk in that I would actually be upping sticks and moving away on my own! All far too quickly I found myself on a ferry to Scotland with some clothes and belongings heading to Stirling in

Scotland to study Business Studies with French. My brother John, who had moved to Scotland a few years previously, was waiting to pick me up at the other side and drive me to my new home! It really had all happened too fast. I had had to say goodbye to my friends and to Charlie. I didn't know when I would see him again. I had very little money and everyone just assumed I would get my university grant very soon. I had decided to take me wee TV with me so, at the last minute, Mum decided to travel in the ferry with me to see me off the other side and then, once in John's safe hands, she would get the ferry straight back again. So that's what happened. It was all a bit surreal to be honest. I was saying goodbye to Mum before I knew what had really hit me. The tears poured down my face. I didn't know what I was doing; I didn't know what I really wanted. But I guessed it was expected of me; to go to university, get a good job, earn loads of money and make the family proud. But the thing is; nobody ever said that. It was the expectations and demands I placed on myself which were the problem.

So here I was being carried away on this self-expectation without neither my heart nor soul really committed to the dream. I had never had the family chat about what was best for me; it just all happened… story of my life, eh!

Not surprisingly I arrived in Stirling and it all went downhill from there. I will not bore you with all the details but suffice to say it was a real mess which didn't help my already fragile mental and physical state. I was incredibly homesick; well, I say 'home' but I mean missing being apart from my Mum and Charlie! The UCAS system had collapsed and Stirling could no longer offer the course I was scheduled to study: instead of studying Business Studies and French they offered me Psychology and Spanish in the first year with a promise that I could transfer over in the second year! Furthermore, due to the crash of the UCAS system too many pupils had been accepted and so there was insufficient accommodation. The student halls were filled to the brim. While I was there I ended up sharing a floor space with another girl in someone else's dorm. I really felt overwhelmed by it all but I tried to stick it out. And as I said before, back in the late eighties there were no other quick forms of communication; no mobile phones or Facebook so students used to queue for literally hours to get to use the public phone boxes on campus. I would get through every day looking forward to speaking to Charlie or my mum.

As days passed, the situation just got worse. When I explained the situation Mum was not very helpful and it seemed she didn't really want me home again. Charlie was dying for me to come home but I was torn. Another battle ensued. Then on top of that I was running out of money; apparently my student grant had gone astray – it really couldn't have got any worse. My efforts to stick it out were at a price. My good friend again stepped in to comfort me. The weight continued to fall off me and my mind was in turmoil. After another few weeks of sheer hell I rang my sister, also living in Scotland, and brother and told them how bad it was. After thinking it all through I gave in – or that is what I told myself I was doing. I was giving in, giving up, failing myself and all those belonging to me. Late one Sunday night my sis arrived with her boyfriend in his car and they packed me and my meagre belongings up and we drove off into the darkness. I left notes for the university professors and the few friends I had made during my time in Stirling, but it was over. I couldn't stay there any longer! Where I was going I wasn't too sure, I still had that to sort! But my episode in Stirling was another one under my belt – another one to beat myself up with! Another painful memory to try to hide along with all the others.

Well, after a few weeks with my sister in Scotland and thinking and talking through my options, I decided to return to Northern Ireland. I had no choice but to go back to the house in Clough. I felt a failure returning after all the goodbyes.

After a short time back I got in touch with the University of Ulster and spoke to a professor there who was Head of European Business Studies with French. I had a good long chat with him, explained the situation to him and he offered me a place on his course starting the following year. I agreed. At least that was something. I tried to convince myself I wasn't a complete failure. Now all that was left was to find out what I was going to do for a year!

Already feeling like a disappointment and still wrecked with the feelings of being a burden back in David's house, I knew I had to try to get a job to keep me going until I went to university. Easier said than done. For a few weeks I walked in and out of town looking for different jobs and going for different interviews. But to no avail. Most said I was overqualified for the typical shop posts I was applying for. By now it was November so luckily shops were starting to recruit Christmas staff. So I got a part-time job for Boots on the tills, doing horrendous Christmas hours but at least I was getting some money. I wanted to be able to give Mum money for the housekeeping! Come January the job came to an end and I was scouring the papers and job centres for work. In between that I was excessively exercising, walking hours on end and trying to keep up my French for university later that year.

As you can imagine, my weight was plummeting but I didn't care, in fact it was my only solace! People started to comment about my size and Mum actually started to tell me off and mentioned it to my sister. By now my periods had stopped for good and in the end I got referred by my GP to the Royal Victoria Hospital, Belfast for an apparent metabolic complaint. I hadn't told my GP the real reason my periods had stopped and why I had lost so much weight. I was still in denial about my illness, I think. The consultant who saw me was an ogre, a horrible man, stuck in the dark ages. He asked me all about my life, my eating and when I gave him a brief overview, which really, looking back I know was my first cry for help, he basically said I was too heavy (at just under seven stone) to be referred to an eating disorder specialist. He basically told me to go away and lose another few pounds if I wanted to get real professional help. I couldn't quite believe my ears. I went home that night, really upset and rang my sister. I didn't really talk to my mum or anyone else for that matter about what was actually happening to me. The secret had to remain that. It was only my secret to tell on a need to know basis. I played it all down with Mum; I didn't want to worry her.

I think it was around that time that I really admitted to myself I had a problem. Up until now I hadn't really thought about it, I was just dealing with everything as best I could. But the penny was starting to drop. I couldn't deny reality any longer. I had anorexia nervosa. That was who my new, secret friend was! But the sad thing is; I didn't care; I didn't want it to stop. I wanted to continue, I wanted to lose more weight. I felt I was doing something I wanted for a change and I was good at it! I had someone or something that was there for me night and day who knew me better than anyone else – how could I give that up? I became obsessed with everything about anorexia nervosa. I went to the local library and ordered all the books I had heard about, such as Susie Orbach's *Fat is a Feminist Issue* and anything else I could get my hands on, on the subject. I could see the librarian looking at me up and down when I submitted quite a long list of books clearly on my eating disorder. I don't think it took Einstein to put the two together. As I have said, there was no Internet or technology at your fingertips so if you wanted to know anything, you had to get books!

So, surprise surprise a few more weeks, maybe two months passed by and I had lost another half stone. At my next appointment with the consultant I basically said "there ya go!" And that was it. However, in order to be referred to one of the top eating disorder specialists in Northern Ireland, Dr Clare Adams, the consultant said I had to first be admitted to hospital. He said I had to stay for at least two weeks and be put on bed rest, and force fed to gain some weight. This was absurd; a few months ago he told me I needed to lose weight to qualify to be 'thin' enough to be referred to get the proper professional help. Now that I have lost that weight I am told I have to be to a medical ward in the Royal Victoria Hospital to gain weight before I can be referred to Dr Adams. Anyway, that was what happened.

I can honestly say it was an awful couple of weeks. I was put in a ward with elderly females. I wasn't allowed out of bed at all for my entire stay, so I had to use commodes and have bed baths. It was all humiliating. At one point I wondered if they were using scare tactics and hoping I would just jump out of bed and say, "that's it; I am cured. Can I go home now?"

I was given huge amounts of food, and not healthy food either; I was given fried eggs and sausages for breakfast, potato dinners, snacks of tea and biscuits two or three times a day. It was awful. My body and mind were going crazy. My friend was horrified. I was betraying her and she was making me feel really guilty. I honestly thought I was going to explode in every way. I hadn't eaten that sort of food in years and my body was reacting as you can imagine. I couldn't wait to get out.

However, while I was there I met a very important person. Someone who would have a strong role in my life for a long time to come: Dr Adams made her first appearance. I knew instantly I was in good hands with her. She was very tall and slim and at once I thought she must at one time have suffered anorexia herself. Surely she couldn't have been so lucky to be that thin naturally? You see, I equated slimness as a very positive trait. To me it signified success, control and beauty. That was what I wanted; that was what I was striving to attain, at all costs. Once the two weeks were over I was discharged. However, despite my desperation to get out of there and get home I didn't really receive a warm reception from anyone. I arrived home to Clough and didn't even say anything about what had happened. As if the past two horrendous weeks spent in hospital being treated as if it was the dark ages never took place. I couldn't speak about it.

My first outpatient appointment with Dr Adams was in August and I recall every second of it. I saw her in her own office in Windsor House, part of the Belfast City hospital. Windsor House, at that time, was an inpatient mental health unit. It housed various patients with mental illnesses not only those with eating disorders. I saw her there once a week for the first few months. Dr Adams went through my entire history just as I have done with you here in this book. She was building her picture of me. Alongside this physical and mental assessment she devised a programme to try to stabilise my weight and my mental state. It started immediately with various medical appointments. I had a number of blood tests and scans taken to ascertain what, if any, damage had been done to my body particularly my internal organs as a result of the anorexia. That was our starting point.

UNIVERSITY LIFE

It was soon time for me to start university. I had kept in touch with a few friends from Victoria College and one of them was studying nursing at the University too. Her parents owned a house in Portland, about six miles from the University and offered me a room in the house. There would be four of us in total sharing 65 Old Coach Road. Obviously I jumped at the chance. It was a much more appealing offer than halls of residence; the memories of Stirling still haunted me.

I had mixed emotions starting university. I was in some ways glad to be doing what I thought I should be; studying and 'bettering' myself! I was also glad to have somewhere which was my mine, well partly – my bedroom was mine – independence for the first time. However, being away from Charlie during the week was quite daunting. After I had come home from Stirling we had grown much closer and I really depended on him. But we said we would see each other every weekend, either he would come to Portland or I would travel back to Clough. Sometimes he even came up for one night a week and stayed over. We had some good times those days. Times when we forgot what my life really was like and we pretended everything was normal and we were just a young couple in love! But my life wasn't normal, we both knew it.

So you will not be surprised to hear that I didn't lead a typical student life. My years at university were spent between studying and Charlie. I never set foot in the

University bar my whole time there! As I didn't eat much or drink at all I was the only student I know who actually saved money on a student grant! I had no other income – I certainly didn't get any financial help from Mum, David or family. Unlike others I was totally on my own. My mum never asked to visit. I was terrified to tell my dad my address, in case one night he would show up drunk as he only lived a few miles away. I felt really guilty about that but I knew that's what I had to do. Otherwise I would be lying in bed worried every time I heard someone staggering or shouting up the street; dreading that drunken bang on the door. I couldn't go through all that again. The scars were still too fresh. I felt like Judas, denying and betraying my own dad. But I knew I had no choice.

Sharing the house with others was also a bit of a challenge. My friend's boyfriend lived in the house too and they would argue loads, often making it a really unpleasant environment to be in. Then there was another Sociology student – she was just the stereotypical student, wasn't really there for an education, more the social life. Appropriate for her degree obviously. While everyone was pleasant enough, having to share a bathroom, a living room and even worse a tiny kitchen with the others was a real challenge for me. I tried to pretend to myself as much as to others that this could work, I could be a normal student and free myself from the shackles of anorexia once and for all. I mixed with other students in the University and in the house – there was no real issue there. Everyone was really friendly and I felt as if I fitted in a wee bit. But I didn't go out socialising or anything: firstly, I didn't drink; secondly I still didn't think I deserved to fully enjoy myself; and thirdly I was saving to get married some day to Charlie. But like all things in my life I threw myself deep into my studies. I felt under extreme pressure to do well; from the previous experiences with Stirling my confidence was at all time low. I was quite worried about how I would cope so I felt I needed to spend every minute studying. Not only did I need to cope I had to be the best – I had to excel this time!

My daily life at this time was extremely demanding and structured. Everything I did was timed to the nth degree and in a particular order; I couldn't handle it otherwise. Every day at uni was the same, the same old routine, a bit like the film *Groundhog Day*. It would start by the dreaded weigh-in. I would leave my shower to afterwards in case this impacted my weight in any way. Perhaps the wet hair would add unwanted ounces?

The amount of stress this one incident caused was inexplicable – it was as if I was in the middle of the MGM Grand Arena in Las Vegas with all eyes on me for the greatest fight on earth. Which side would win? The shouts would be deafening but the shouts were in my head and there was no one else only me – my two sides fighting the bit out was enough! The thing was I could never win, I would always lose… a never-ending battle. I would stand on the scales with my eyes tight closed dreading any gain in weight from the day before. Even the minutest fraction of an ounce would matter; it would mean I had failed from the day before. At that very second this was the most dominant and key thing in my world. Nothing else mattered… Looking back this seems so unbelievable and to many readers this seems absurd. But for me, and anyone else who has suffered from anorexia, that was the reality; that summed up my life then! And those times when my secret friend got her way; when I had lost weight, even an ounce, I felt jubilant. All was well in the world. I felt I had achieved something and I was in control. My friend knew what was best for me and I was living the dream.

Once I had weighed myself I quickly updated my diary with what I had eaten the day before, what I weighed and any key information. Not the usual type of diary but worth its weight (no pun intended) in gold to me. At this stage I was about six stone and struggling to keep going... I would hate myself each time I saw the scales and realised I hadn't lost any weight since the day before – what a lazy bitch! What a greedy cow, and God help me if I had gained even the smallest ounce. The mental torture would be unbearable. I would feel ashamed, a failure, lazy, guilty and the self-hatred would be all-consuming. I would quickly tell myself I had to do better today. I could hardly sleep at night worried about what the scales would tell me the next morning. It was a never-ending battle – the only way to feel better was to lose more weight, I told myself, but I never did. I never felt better no matter how little I weighed, my friend was moving the goalposts all the time! Deep down I knew this was a battle I could never win, but I knew I was already caught up in the whirlwind and couldn't let go.

After this daily torture I would then get showered, dressed and ready for university. Most of my house mates would also be up by then and mulling around downstairs in the kitchen and sitting room.

Even though I felt I didn't deserve anything to eat, hey! I had been lying still all night, burning no calories whatsoever, so what had I done to earn anything to eat? Yes, that was the type of thing went through my head constantly. Anyway I knew the deal with Dr Adams was I had to have some breakfast. In fact we had a sort of agreed menu which I really was supposed to stick to as best I could. It was in fact my 'Licence to Eat'! Yes you heard right: Dr Adams actually wrote me out a licence, like a driving licence which said, "I, Ali North deserved, was allowed and had to eat the following things each day... " and it would have listed the various bits of food I had begrudgingly agreed I would try and stomach.

During the depths of my illness, , the trauma of deciding whether I was allowed or should eat, whether I should allow myself to rest, exercise or even sleep… in fact any decision where I was torn because of my illness and secret friend had become too overwhelming. Common sense and normality do not exist with anorexia. My two sides would fight about whether I should eat or not, a real domestic would be going on in my head. The result was I couldn't even make, never mind feel inner contentment about, even the slightest decision without extreme distress. So Dr Adams decided she would issue me licenses which entitled me to the most basic human rights. Then I would keep the licences on me at all times, in the knowledge that Dr Adams said it was OK to eat! I know to some this may sound absurd but let me tell you, in many dark hours this got me through. The fact that someone else, someone who you genuinely trusted and you truly believed was concerned for your well-being was telling you that you needed and, more importantly, deserved to do something, was invaluable! When really desperate I would read and re-read the licence, trying to convince myself of the words:

"That I, Ali North, was allowed and deserved to eat…"

I tried to convince myself that it wasn't me being greedy or eating just because I wanted to. I was told I had to. The key thing here was the good Ali, the obedient child stepped in and that side of me knew I had to obey!

So, once this daily drama was over I could then head downstairs to the extremely small kitchen and prepare my breakfast tray. I had my own bowl, cup and teapot. Everything was laid out to precision. I put the exact measure of all bran into the bowl. If I had time I would have probably counted the bits to be sure it was same amount every day! I made a pot of weak black tea – one tea bag only. Then I made a jug of watered-down milk. There was no dining area and so I had to go into the sitting room to eat. The others would be wondering in and out, the TV would be on and I found the whole atmosphere extremely unnerving. When I had to eat, I needed to have total peace and quiet, with no one moving about. I couldn't have anyone talk to me or interrupt me – so I sat in the corner in my usual chair with no one beside me and proceeded to eat my feast, or so it felt.

The strange thing is while I was terrified of eating and the consequences it brought (well, the exaggerated irrational consequences in my head anyway) deep down the hungry, vulnerable child part of me was literally crying out for food and nourishment. That part of me looked forward to sitting down to eat. That part of me didn't want to be interrupted by anyone, they wanted to enjoy the food and lap it all up. The fear overhung however that once that meek child started eating they would never stop the hunger was so great. Yet I know now, the physical deprivation was symbolic of the emotional starvation – which is not quite as easy to satisfy after years of neglect. While I ate I felt like all eyes were on me. Every mouthful was accompanied with extremely negative thoughts and emotions. Sometimes I even had to fight back the tears just to get through a meal.

Once breakfast was over I would clean up and get ready to catch the bus. I attended all my classes and lectures at university – I told you before I was the model student. In the breaks between lectures I headed to the library or the gym – the others headed to the coffee bar or the student union, later in the day. However, I wasn't allowed to do any of that, my friend would tell me. The dominating thoughts were constant. I wasn't allowed to relax and hang out with the others. I had to keep working, pushing the mind and punishing the body.

While I was friendly with almost everyone in my degree year I wasn't really close to anyone. I needed my own space, I couldn't let the real me be known. I had to keep my secret safe. While they went one direction I would head off to the library to get ahead in the homework or just do extra studying. If I had more time to spare I would visit the gym. I would carry my gym bag with me just in case an unexpected opportunity arose. I would run on the treadmill for ages and push myself through a real thorough workout. During the day I didn't eat at all. I only allowed myself diet coke. That would keep me going until night-time. As you can imagine, this wasn't part of the licence agreement! Then at the end of the day I might decide to walk into Ballydunn town centre and get the bus home from there – the mind had quickly calculated that would be an extra thirty minutes of exercise and more calories burnt off. At that time, my brother Jack lived in the town and so I sometimes called there to see him and his family. I did miss Mum and Charlie so often it served as a pick-me-up. Sometimes in the winter the weather was so bad Jack just got me to stay the night rather than me have to travel back to Portland in the harsh conditions. I was extremely frail back then. Not that I could see it of course, but looking back I know I was, and I was often literally blue with the cold. I could never wear enough layers to heat me and I was obviously worried about how enormous I looked with so many pieces of clothing on, too. I knew my family was genuinely worried about my failing health.

But most days after university I just headed to the house in Portland. I would light the coal fire for the others coming in and get stuck into my studies.

Dinner time would be another extremely stressful ritual. From the time I got home I would be starting to inwardly panic about what time I should eat, wondering what time the others would get in, what time they would be in the kitchen. My mind would get so carried away that I really couldn't concentrate too much on my studies until the dirty deed was done! Then the argument in my head would start about whether I should just go without any dinner to save any guilt or embarrassment. Sometimes the anorexic side won and I went without anything further to eat or drink until the next day. I would go to bed feeling physically starving but mentally victorious, looking forward to the next morning's weigh-in to see if I had been rewarded by my abstinence. I wasn't always! The kitchen was extremely small so I had to try to perfect the execution so I had enough time in it alone to prepare the feast and eat it. Hard task when students just come and go without any apparent rhyme or reason. Obviously my house-mates were not aware of the importance of every part of my regimented routine and so didn't know that if they came into the kitchen to chat and genuinely be friendly while I was preparing my, again, very routinely laid-out salad that they were causing me extreme stress. They weren't to know that if they happened to come into the kitchen while I was, as usual, sitting facing the wall on the small stool at the breakfast bar trying to swallow every mouthful of my plateful of grass that I was literally being eaten up inside with feelings of guilt at having been caught eating. But yet at the same time I felt like a dog with a bone in case someone would take my plate away, as I needed and deep down yearned for the nourishment! How would anyone know that? How would anyone know what devastating impact they could have by simply speaking to me while I was eating?

I looked forward to the evening – night-time was more peaceful and it meant I had survived another day! I knew I didn't have to listen to the fights within my head when I was sleeping. I didn't have any university social life in the evenings, or at any time for that matter. The others would often go out to Kelly's or some other local bar. They would invite me but I never went. I enjoyed having the house to myself: the peace, the sanctity of my own space. But the double-edged sword was I was actually scared of being by myself. I didn't trust my two sides. I felt scared to be on my own with my friend. She was too evil to me and I didn't want to have to listen to her any more, I was both physically and mentally drained by it all.

At the weekends or holidays, I usually went back to Clough, to see Mum and Charlie. The odd time I would stay in Portland and Charlie would come down. But, my secret friend was there all the time – I was never on my own in a nice, calming way. She dictated everything. She never left me. No matter where I was I had to fit in a certain amount of exercise, I would have a few walks with Charlie, and I would normally study. Oh, and at some point I would eat the usual controlled, pathetic morsels. No wild parties or student life for me. I still didn't drink alcohol at all, too many calories of course!

By this stage in my illness I had become really irrational about how I looked or what others thought about me or how they saw me. This is typical of the illness. My self-images were all distorted. I felt fat and, to me, looked it! Sometimes I even thought I could see myself growing before my very eyes. I hated mirrors – they were like torture. Similar to the scales they would never tell me or show me what I wanted to see. I couldn't bear for my clothes to feel tight on me, they would act as a constant reminder that I must be too fat. Logic no longer existed in anything I did. So I bought smaller clothes to punish myself even further; it meant I had to lose more weight so they would feel looser. It was a horrendous spiral of torture and demands.

My mind was so preoccupied with my anorexia and my friend; it was like a full-time job in itself. I was so committed to it, to her, I couldn't let them down. And added to that, the lack of food and extreme physical exercise regimes I would put myself through made it extremely challenging to concentrate on my degree – but I somehow did.

During my first year at university Charlie and I got engaged. It was very exciting and romantic. We picked the ring and he formally proposed to me on my twentieth birthday on bended knee on the steps of a church we hoped one day we would get married in. The church was in the quaint village of Erin where we would often take leisurely romantic walks. I remember the day vividly. I wore a green polo neck under a black trouser suit; very elegant. While it was April the Northern Irish weather can literally treat you to four seasons in one day. Furthermore, I was extremely frail by this stage so always felt the cold. We then popped into the Country House to show my mum the ring, have a coffee and head away for the day. But even on such a special day of our engagement the friend had to come along too. Always there by my side, whether wanted or not. So we went to a beautiful hotel in the lakes to have a fancy meal to celebrate; you know the usual thing people do but, obviously, with me it wasn't the straightforward, relaxing experience it should have been! But Charlie seemed to enjoy it. For a short time, before my friend started bellowing in my head, I did feel a little special that day; I did feel wanted and loved.

DR ADAMS

Every Friday afternoon I would get the train from university, get off in Belfast, walk to the hospital with my heavy bags, see Dr Adams and then Charlie would pick me up afterwards. It became a weekly routine for us all. Dr Adams would help me enough to get through the next week and ensure I had sufficient medication. I was on strong painkillers and anti-depressants at that time. I could unload all the rubbish in my head, I would share my diary contents with her, talk through the anguish of my very being. Just to say it all out loud helped a bit – you couldn't just say that stuff to just anyone. I know how weird and crazy it all sounds so I could only ever let those words out my mouth to the ears of a professional. Dr Adams would analyse what I said and together we would try and work through it all. Not easy. She would also do something else for me, remember, she would give me that valuable 'licence to eat'! I look forward to seeing that James Bond movie!

    I would come out of each session mentally drained but it would get me through to the next time. As time progressed in my first year at university we often spoke of me being admitted to Windsor House and treated as an inpatient instead. Dr Adams thought I should – she really felt I needed to get constant help and while the weekly outpatient sessions were better than nothing, she felt real progress would only come from being admitted. It was quite a dilemma and one I had to make. Like every question, from the smallest to the most significant, my mind struggled to cope, the two sides fought about the right decision. Did I really want help? Of course my secret friend said no. She felt under threat. Did I really want to get rid of the only thing I really knew that I could control and trust? Did I want to lose that and give up that relationship? What would I be like without her? It was too scary to even contemplate. But somewhere very deep down there was this little voice begging for help, begging for a small morsel of food, for rest, to be free from the constant mental and physical torture once and for all. What should I do? I needed someone to make that decision for me. It turned out Dr Adams did that: she took the decision out of my hands and decided I needed to be admitted.

WINDSOR HOUSE

I did not want my university degree to be impacted in any way nor did I want word of my illness to get out to my peers' circle. My secret had to be protected at all costs. If I was to go into hospital it would have to be during the summer after I finished my first year. So it was agreed, on Monday 5 June I would be admitted to Windsor House for as long as it took – whether it would be days, weeks or months.

Looking back the situation was very similar to many big events in my past such as when Mum and I fled from Ballydunn or when I went off to university in Scotland and so on. I just went with it without allowing myself to feel! So this was to be no different. No one was to know about me going into hospital and I had to keep the big secret all to myself. Breaking up with university friends for the summer was similarly tinged with poignancy, many heading off for a holiday in the sun, some heading off to work for the summer and then me – heading into hospital to try to fight my secret demons!

The timing was strange too because Charlie was heading away to camp with the UDR for a week the Saturday before. I had to say my goodbyes to him early on the Saturday morning; that was very tearful, he was a very emotional, romantic guy. On the Monday morning I was getting myself a taxi to the hospital once Mum and David had gone to work. I did not want to make a fuss, I was pretending to everyone, including myself that it wasn't happening.

When I arrived at Windsor House I didn't really know what to expect. As I say it all happened without me allowing myself to think too much about it. Obviously, my secret friend was furious as if I was betraying her, trying to free myself from her evil grip.

Anyway, once I was formally admitted by Dr Adams and my care nurse, Jackie, I was taken to the ward which was to become my new home for the next while. Now I knew the ward was not solely for anorexics. I knew it was a mental health unit so females with various illnesses would reside there at any one time. However, it was for long-stay patients not just for someone needing treatment for a night or two. At the other end of the wing was the unit for mentally ill male patients. Walking into the ward it suddenly hit me where I was and what was happening. I saw straight away Liz, who was obviously suffering from an eating disorder. She looked so thin. It is strange because I now know that I was actually frailer than Liz at that stage but my illness prevented me from seeing the truth.

Liz spoke to me immediately. The other 'roommates' are always given a heads-up when a new patient is being admitted. Liz was very friendly and welcoming. Jackie let me have a quick chat with her before moving me to my bed. I can still picture it now. The beds either side of mine were empty, which was great. The bed opposite me belonged to a girl called Judith, another eating disorder victim, around my age. She was much quieter and shyer than Liz. Judith kept her belongings very tidy; in fact there was a very clinical, austere look to her bed space. On the other hand Liz, in her mid/late twenties, had her area decorated with blankets, cushions, photos and personal touches – it was like a real home although somewhat childish in appearance for a woman of her age. Not much wonder, I later learnt she had been in Windsor House for two years and there was no sign of her going anywhere. Judith had just arrived two weeks before me. While I was in Windsor House I made friends with both girls but I became particularly close to Judith; we had much more similar traits, I thought. We were the three anorexics in our unit.

For the first few days it felt like I was on a school trip. It was all new and I was meeting new people; new doctors, new nurses, and obviously other patients. I had said strictly from the outset that the only person I wanted to have to step inside that place was Charlie; no other visitors at all. And that wish was obeyed. I didn't have any visitors that first week in hospital until Charlie returned from camp.

But after a few days reality struck and I realised that I was in a mental health unit! What had I done? Why had I agreed to do this? My secret friend was not happy. Her every existence was being challenged and forced to shut up.

From very early on an eating plan had been devised for me. Well they said we 'Planned it together' but really? The dietician would sit and explain all the vitamins and nutrients I so badly needed and tried to incorporate as many as possible into my new, healthy eating regime. What a laugh, I used to sit and listen to them all, trying to give them the respect they deserved, but inwardly my friend would snigger as I knew inside out about vitamins, and calorific content… I had read every article about the matter – how else did I know how to avoid them and beat the system?

From the outset of anyone suffering from anorexia nervosa, treatment was usually focused on the physical. It seemed the answer was simple! Eat more, gain weight, there you go, problem solved! Now why didn't I think of that?

This was the predominant form of treatment used to 'shake some sense' into the majority of sufferers either as outpatients or inpatients. Patients would be fed high-fat, high-calorie diets, possibly even force fed if thought necessary. They would have been put them on bed rest with severe activities restricted. So naturally the end result over time would be weight gain but at the cost of the patient's sanity! Not only does this torture the mind but visibly the patient feels themselves growing before their very own eyes. Furthermore, their stomachs have shrunk through months, maybe years of eating little so it is physically impossible to start eating considerably larger amounts of food on a regular basis without your body reacting in the form of nausea, diarrhea and general feeling of illness.

Now let me stress I totally understand in many cases when the patient is dangerously underweight that the physical attention has to be the priority for two reasons; one, in the extreme cases the life has to be saved; and secondly, if the brain is not fed and in a healthier state it cannot function and rational about the patient's true condition is even harder to achieve.

Linked to these various harsh treatments would be the prescription drugs, which would range from various kinds of antidepressants to relaxants and sedatives. While I was in hospital, drugs round dished out quite a party mix sometimes. Thirty years on I still take quite a high dosage of daily medication.

When I started in Windsor House I was also given a timetable showing the therapy sessions and various medical appointments I had to attend each week; some on an individual basis and some in groups. I initially hated the group therapies as I hated to talk about me and my friend; it had all been my secret for so long that I just couldn't let anyone in. I largely listened and my eyes were truly opened by the lives and experiences of my fellow inpatients. People do not realise the true horror of those suffering from a mental illness. There were set mealtimes and all patients ate together in the dining room. It was like a big school hall with all the kids lining up for their food. Like the others with eating disorders, I hated that bit most of all; I found it extremely hard to deal with. The nurses would be walking around checking you were eating your food, noting up your records. Then they followed you around after mealtimes to ensure you didn't visit the bathrooms to throw it up again. It started to feel like I was in prison. It was there in Windsor House that I promised myself I would write a book, and what do you know? Lol!

Aside from the rigid mealtimes, the therapy classes, counselling and medical check-ups I was left to my own devices. I could read, watch TV or whatever. Having said that, most days were quite full on; it was more the evenings and weekends that I had more free time. After a while I started to question what I was doing. Charlie would come and visit me as often as he could and I felt so guilty that we should be out together having fun and instead here he was visiting me, in a mental health hospital!

Then there were the dreaded hospital weigh-ins. As I have already touched on, it is very hard to explain how this seemingly simple event injected such fear and worry into someone, but these did. Again it was a double-edged sword because I knew that if I had not gained any weight or met my target weight for the day or week I would have been punished by having more mobility restricted and calorie intake increased – both horror to an anorexic's ears. But on the other hand if you had gained even an ounce I knew how horribly guilt-ridden and disgusted I would feel about myself. This in turn would have driven me into deeper depression. It was a vicious circle. One I knew I couldn't win. The night before the weigh-ins I wouldn't sleep with panic over what the morning would bring. For many the only option was to cheat. So how do you do that? Well, some would try to drink as much water as possible immediately beforehand. Others would actually have small stones or paperweights which they would try to disguise in their underwear. That's how bad this was and how horrendous the impact was on you. However, the nurses were aware of all the tricks of the trade and often searched you as much as was decently possible for any hidden, weighty tools!

I must admit when I was in Windsor I saw things which I wish I hadn't. Memories that will always stay with me, and not good ones! For some of the other mentally ill patients they received treatment in the form of Electroconvulsive Therapy, known as ECT. You are familiar with Frankenstein and the image of his head being zapped by electric currents? Well hard to believe it but this type of treatment is still used in this twenty-first century! At least this treatment realised the problem had something to do with the mind, albeit it was severe in the extreme, archaic and horrific to undergo and witness. During one of my hospital spells I vividly remember other patients being prepped for, and then returning from, ECT. They were like zombies afterwards, I'm not joking. But they never remembered anything about it. We would often look down the hospital corridor where the ECT treatment was being carried out and see extreme lights flashing as volts were being charged. I must admit it still horrifies me to this day.

All these treatments methods have been, and in many places continue to be used. The problem with such extreme methods is that the aim is to cure the patient in an unnatural and speedy manner. The missed point and the key to the comprehension of this illness is that the physical state is the result of the mental. The real treatment needs to tackle the mind. Once that is treated, the body can follow.

Throughout my time in Windsor House my secret friend would make me question whether being in hospital was benefitting me at all. As the months passed and we were at the end of August I had to seriously think of what I was going to do regarding university. The second year began in the middle of September with two weeks spent studying in Lyons, in the south of France.

So I had to evaluate what I had achieved during my stay and whether I should remain for another while or should I be discharged and return to university. Big decision and you know I am not great at them. So I did talk it through with my sister Susan, Charlie and obviously my nurses and Dr Adams. Sorry, I think I forgot to mention, Susan had been a rock of support throughout my stay in Windsor, ringing me most nights at nine p.m. for a quick update. She knew my circumstances best out of all my family members and had a nursing background, remember. In the end, I looked back over the three months in Windsor and summed up what had happened: I had tried. I had obeyed the doctors and nurses by being admitted and for following their rules for my duration. I had gained a little weight, but only a few pounds: quite surprising considering the regime I had to undergo. So I was almost six and a half stone by then. But it was all at a price. I had stopped living my normal life; I had seen things I didn't want to see any more. I wanted control back. My friend had had enough. So, I agreed to be discharged on 2 September; to give me a few days with Mum and Charlie before heading to Lyons and resuming student life. I couldn't wait to get out, then. Had there been any point in going into Windsor House? Had I fought the demons? Had I got rid of my friend? No! But I did it; I survived and lived to tell the tale!

UNIVERSITY – SECOND YEAR

So oblivious to all my university friends and professors I met them in Belfast International Airport in September and we flew to Lyons to spend two weeks studying at the University of Lyons and having business meetings at some of the most prestigious companies there.

My secret life was evident from the outset of that gathering at the airport. As stories were told of summer holidays and jobs, I kept quiet with memories soaring through my head of what I had done and seen since May! The secret had to remain that.

Lyons was OK. Another good experience from a student point of view, but my friend came with me as usual.

The rest of my second year was very much like my first. I went back to the same student house with the same housemates. I studied, exercised, ate very little and any little weight gained in Windsor had been quickly lost again; much to my friend's satisfaction. In fact, I had to buy a rubber ring so I could take a bath as my butt was so bony by that stage, I was no fat-bottomed girl, that was for sure!

I continued seeing Dr Adams on a weekly basis and basically she just kept me alive.

CAR ACCIDENT

Unfortunately that Christmas something horrific happened. Charlie and I were on the way to Ballydunn in the car the day before Christmas Eve to deliver Christmas presents to my family. It was about six p.m. and we were approaching a wee village just outside called Bannhall. There were no streetlights and it was pitch black outside in the depth of winter. We were both in the Christmas mood and Charlie had now finished work for the holidays. We were chatting and singing along to the radio when suddenly all I felt was this sudden gust of wind, there was a loud thump and the sound of breaking glass. Charlie slammed on the brakes and with the tires screeching we came to a sudden stop. It was all so sudden, seconds only yet it changed our lives forever. I felt wetness in the dark and suddenly I realised what had happened. There was a human body on my lap. We had hit someone! It was like an awful nightmare. I started screaming. I am not exactly sure what happened next but I know I pulled myself from the car dragging my legs from underneath the body. A few cars had stopped and people came running over to me. It was all a bit of a blur. I don't even know where Charlie was at this stage. Then I took a look, I had to see. I walked to the front of the car and there I saw the damage – the car was mangled and this unknown person's body was half on the bonnet and half on top of the passenger's seat where I had been. I passed out. The next thing I recall was being in an ambulance with Charlie. We were taken to the nearest

Casualty and both treated immediately for extreme shock. I also had quite severe trauma to my left leg and several cuts to my hands and legs. I think the steering wheel saved Charlie from any real physical damage and his side of the car had not been impacted the way the passenger side had. We were lucky to be alive considering, the doctors kept telling us.

The police were there to initially question us and explain they would take witness statements from us the following day when we would hopefully be less distressed. They said they would take the car to the police station for analysis in case the car had been unroadworthy, but it seemed that it had just been a terrible accident. They explained that the victim had been an elderly lady suffering from Alzheimer's who lived with her family in Bannhall. Unfortunately, somehow she got out of the house by herself and had wandered through the fields. She literally came out of nowhere and stepped onto the road. We couldn't have seen her. It was completely dark, she was wearing dark clothing and she came out of the hedge along the road into the path of our car on my side. It could have happened to anyone, but it happened to us.

By the time we had arrived at hospital the police had notified my next of kin and my brother and his wife were waiting inside for us. When we eventually got discharged in the early hours of the following morning, Christmas Eve by that stage, they took us back to their house. My sister-in-law had bought me some clothes as mine had been all torn and bloodstained. They had been binned by the medical staff. I remember sitting in an armchair in my brother's house, numb. I didn't want to go to bed; I knew I wouldn't sleep. I was scared to close my eyes because I feared what I would see. I couldn't speak. Then I heard the local news on the TV – and there it was; the words shot though my very core, the newsreader said as plain as day, "An elderly lady has been killed in a road traffic accident outside Bannhall. One car was involved. The driver and front seat passenger in the car have now been discharged from hospital with minor injuries. It is feared the deceased had stepped in front of the vehicle." The fatal words kept going through my head like a broken record. I kept hearing, *"an elderly lady had been killed"*. That was our fault – we did that. I would have to be punished; I would suffer for that. And with that the anorexia took a tighter grip.

The impact this accident had on us both was significant but not surprisingly more on me than Charlie. My already hardened feelings of guilt and unworthiness were exacerbated with the disturbing knowledge *'we had killed someone'*.

I got through the rest of my second year at university as best I could. I was finding it extremely difficult to cope with my illness and continue with my education, but I had no choice. I had to! I deserved to be punished, my friend said…

BELGIUM

The third year of my university degree was my 'year abroad'. In August that year I received notification from my professor that I had been given a place at a university in the south of Belgium called Louvain-la-Neuve. They spoke French there and the purpose of the third year of my European Business Studies degree was to live and work in a French-speaking country, so that year Belgium was the chosen destination. The other students in my year had all been sent to Liège together but for some reason I was chosen to go to Louvain-la-Neuve on my own! Like many times in my life before, the fact that I was heading off to study in Belgium for a year hadn't really sunk in as I was saying my goodbyes to family and Charlie at the airport. I just acted without too much thought. It was easier that way, it meant I didn't have to feel or succumb to any real emotions.

Back then there were no direct flights to Brussels from Northern Ireland so I had to take two flights and transfer through Heathrow. I eventually arrived in Louvain-la-Neuve after an extremely long day and then had to go through the complicated admission process, in French of course! I was allocated a room in a *kot* – the name for a student house there. My *kot* was quite a walk from the main university campus up an extremely steep cobblestoned hill. I eventually found it in the dark and hauled my heavy suitcases up to the top floor. Of course, I had been given the room at the top of the house and it definitely wasn't the penthouse suite. Don't get me wrong the rooms were fine, very basic but clean. Looking back I am not quite sure how I even managed to drag those heavy suitcases that distance; I was only about five and a half stone at that stage.

The other five Belgian students moved in over the next few days and I introduced myself to them whenever I bumped into them. Four of them were really close friends; two girls and two guys. I think they were having relationships with one another but it was never always clear who was with whom. The fifth housemate was a sweet girl. She was very friendly and I think she was very sympathetic to my situation. She didn't stay all the time mind you, but when she did she always knocked on my door for a wee chat to check I was OK. I think she quickly realised I was very homesick and had issues, let's say, as she would often bring me snacks and home-cooked treats.

I must admit after the initial settling-in period was well and truly over and I knew my way about the university campus reality started to hit me! I was hundreds of miles away from home and everyone belonging to me. I suddenly felt really alone. May I remind you, this was the early 1990s so there were no mobile phones or similar technology? Plus money was scarce and so I couldn't even ring home from a phone box too often. If you wanted to communicate with loved ones you had to resort to pen and paper, imagine that. I did receive the odd letter from back home which sometimes brightened me up. But the sad thing was if I got the letter in the morning I would not open it straightaway. I would carry it about all day and when I got home, leave it on my pillow. The thought of that letter kept me going many a day. I would then settle into bed at night and excitedly open and read my wee letter. I would usually get extremely tearful and therefore I could just cry myself to sleep afterwards. Mum didn't really write letters, they were usually from Charlie. He wrote almost every week, bless him. My dad and Granny O'Hara wrote me a few letters during my time there even though their handwriting was hard to make out sometimes. In fact, I have kept them all. But it was the association and reminders of home that the letters represented. Looking back I really was extremely homesick and depression was setting in but, me, being me I was in complete denial. I would get through; I had to do this no matter how I felt physically or emotionally. But I had no means of help out there. I felt truly isolated from everything and everyone.

From Monday to Friday I went to my lessons, all in French, without really talking to anyone. At the weekends I spent most of my time alone too. I would lie in bed to noon just to get the time in. Occasionally I would chat with the other students in my *kot* and sometimes I would take myself off to visit another part of Belgium such as Bruges or Antwerp in the north, of Belgium, where Flemish was spoken (a bit like German or Dutch) not French. I really felt very vulnerable those months – like a little lost soul with no one in the world to care for them. And I looked forward to the occasional phone call back home; I would speak to Mum and Charlie as often as my money would allow.

Not surprisingly, my eating habits were deteriorating as well. I was down to eating just once a day; in the evening about seven-ish. I was also starting to adopt extreme quirks around mealtime; it became a really OCD affair. I found it hard because I had to make the dinner in the kitchen which was always a hive of activity because, not only were my house-mates there most of the time, but some of their friends hung out at ours too! They would often comment, in French, sometimes to me and sometimes behind my back – little did they know my hearing was excellent and my French obviously better than they gave me credit for. They would mention how thin I was and comment on my plate of boiled vegetables and fruit – yes, boiled vegetables and fruit. Every night at the same time made with the same military precision! Then off to my room to eat it – they couldn't understand why I couldn't just sit at the table amongst all their shouting and carrying on and eat my meal. Well, to me and to many similar sufferers that would be totally out of the question. No, I had to hide away in my room and eat in silence, alone and deal with the guilt, greed and disgust I felt while having my only food of the day. Once I had done the deed and cleaned up I would get sorted for my bed, trying to bring another lonely day to close. I fretted quite a bit; I felt like a prisoner counting the days until I would get home again.

So taking into account my extreme anxiety, low mood, the loneliness, the distance I used to walk to and from campus several times a day and the little food I was eating, it is not surprising that over a few weeks I had lost almost another stone in weight.

The strange thing was, as I was out there sharing a room in a house with other Belgians, I did not have my own personal scales so I wasn't able to weigh myself daily like I had been back home. I wasn't actually aware of what weight I was which was scary and hard for me to deal with in itself. I often had nightmares that I had gained lots of weight and looked enormous. The first time my recent weight loss really came to my attention was the morning I was heading to Brussels to meet my other student friends staying in Liège and our university professor visiting us from home. I remember putting on a skirt – a rare event I can assure you – and some hold-up tights. Well they didn't! I had lost so much weight from my legs that the hold-ups were not doing their job and kept falling to my ankles! Not a pretty sight when running for my train. I had to use emergency safety pins to get through the day. I couldn't understand at first; I thought the elastic had gone... and then I realised. My immediate thought was of elation... then quickly followed with thoughts on how I was going to get through the day in one of the major fashion capitals of the world without doing a Nora Batty impression.

When I arrived at the Brussels office I could tell my friends and the professor were shocked to see me. I didn't catch on why at the start, but I later found out they saw how much weight I had lost since we had last met and I looked, in their words, like 'death warmed up'. It is only now when I see a photo of myself in those days that I can see what others saw – I couldn't then! But that's what happens. When you are in the depths of anorexia you lose all logic and sense of reality – you literally cannot see how you actually look. Your self-images are so distorted that in your eyes you look huge. It is a bit like those crazy mirrors you see at the funfair which make you look all weird – sometimes really tall or squashed. Well, that is often what an anorexic experiences when they see themselves in the mirror, only they cannot depict the truth from the distortion.

Around this time I started to get really sharp pains in my right knee. They got so bad that at one point I literally had to drag my right leg to be able to move about. I must admit I must have looked a sorry sight. The pain became so unbearable that I ended up going to the doctor on the university campus. Despite his broken English and my lack of French medical vocabulary we both understood what was going on. He was so nice and strongly advised I get an urgent scan done by another specialist in a nearby town. He kindly made a few calls and I had an appointment later that afternoon. I had to literally drag myself on and off two buses and walk a fair bit to get to the appointment. But I did it. And of course I had to pay for all this as there is no NHS equivalent in Belgium. Mind you the doctor I first saw didn't charge me; I think he generally felt so sorry for me. I explained I was a visiting student in Louvain-la-Neuve and that I had no family or even close friends. I suspect he guessed the underlying medical issues aside from my knee problem.

The scan showed that at least nothing was broken but that I had the early stages of osteoporosis; obviously as a result of my anorexia – so that wasn't good. However, the specialist thought the current pain was likely from gout. Now many of you might be saying, "Nonsense, surely gout is a middle-aged man's illness due to a rich gentrified lifestyle of excessive red meat and red wine! However, while this may have been the stereotypical case many years ago others can get it, too! Gout is a type of arthritis caused by having too much of the chemical, uric acid, in your bloodstream. If levels of uric acid are high for prolonged periods, needle-like crystals can start to form in your tissues, resulting in swollen, painful joints. So this is what had happened to me. I think it was a mixture of my kidneys not working efficiently, my further weight loss and diet high in tomatoes and apples and very little else (although there is no medical evidence why these would have that effect but it was suggested they were the dietary culprit in my case). And too much walking! The consultant prescribed me strong painkillers, steroids, an anti-inflammatory and rest. The pain started to ease after a few weeks but it was still problematic for many years. It never stopped me doing anything, mind you, and like many things I just learned to live with it. To me it was further punishment I had to endure. My so-called friend was giving me hell.

By this stage I had become so homesick that I booked flights for a long weekend – my first time home since August and I was so excited. No one could pick me up at the airport so I just got a taxi to Mum's house and Charlie was meeting me there once he got off work. It was so good to be home; I knew I only had five days but I would make the most of it. Everyone was immediately horrified when they saw me – they couldn't hide it in their faces. I couldn't understand it of course, I didn't know how different I looked to them. Although, looking back, I know I looked extremely ill. I literally looked as if I was at death's door. Once I told Dr Adams I was back for a few days she gave me an immediate appointment. I was desperate to see her, to offload all my bottled-up issues over the last few months and get some urgent medication to see me through to the next visit home, which would probably be Christmas. My appointment with Dr Adams was a lifesaver and I do not use that term lightly. Dr Adams too expressed her shock on how ill I looked and, coming from her, I sat up and took notice more. Coincidentally I took really physically ill in her office with sharp, shooting pains in my abdomen. She drove me immediately to the Royal Victoria Hospital in Belfast and got me an emergency appointment. Apparently I was extremely low in various minerals and was given urgent IV fluids. I got out later that night. During my appointment and my unexpected trip to the hospital Dr Adams and I talked at length about the next few months. Her strong medical advice was that I had to stay at home and not return to Belgium. She suggested I take a break from university for another year to get on top of things again. She thought I was rapidly deteriorating and that I may not survive another few months out there. But, as usual, I couldn't accept the seriousness of the situation. I lived in third party mode – strongly displaying the 'Don't be silly, I will be fine, this isn't happening to me' attitude.

I didn't say too much about what Dr Adams warned me to anyone else. Better they didn't know. It did play around in my head but I just couldn't believe I was that ill. I just couldn't pull out of university – I couldn't be responsible for being such a failure! As the day to go back got closer I was filled with dread. I hated the thought of going back to my lonely existence in Belgium. This time I knew what was there and how desperate I felt. The morning I was due to fly back, the house phone rang and I was very surprised to hear Dr Adams on the phone. I still cannot believe it to this day; but she was *begging* me not to go back. She was genuinely concerned; this was not a routine call from your normal NHS Dr. She had rung me at six a.m. in her own time as she had been thinking about me all night. She warned me of the possible consequences. So guess what I did? I ignored them – and I got on that flight. I was more heavy-hearted than in August but that bitch was dragging me back to Belgium – maybe she wanted me dead once and for all. And I couldn't fight her, so I got on that plane.

I arrived back to Belgium to find I had achieved excellent exam results for the oral university tests I had taken a few weeks previous and consequently the offer of a post in the European Commission – Wow! However, a few days later I received a letter from my university head Professor O'Brien basically saying that they were pulling me out of Belgium before I "came home in a coffin". Yip, that is what he wrote. Apparently the university professor who had been over had gone back and reported how ill I was and that, if anything happened to me, it would the university's responsibility. So for my and their benefit, I had to return home immediately. I was distraught – they couldn't do this to me. I had no one to turn to. I didn't know what to do. I had messed up big time, I had failed. It was out of my hands now, I had no option but to go home and make an appointment to see them over my future at university. I made a quick call home and told Mum and Charlie what had happened and I was coming home. They were delighted! I booked my flights for 10 December and began packing up all my belongings. Deep down I was relieved. This part of my life was over and I hadn't given in. The decision had been made for me, I just needed to figure out what happened next. I couldn't wait to get home.

My university professor arranged for me to meet him at the start of 1991 to discuss my options. With great anxiety and a heavy heart I met him. I had no choice but to be completely honest and fill him in on my background. I explained that since my return from Belgium Dr Adams and I had agreed an intensive recovery programme to address both the most urgent physical and psychological issues. Well, he was brilliant, very supportive. It was the best thing I could have done.

He promised to do all he could to help me finish my degree as planned.

He agreed to obtain written reports from my Belgian professors at Louvain-La-Neuve to cover the academic part of my third year. I would have been due to finish at the end of January anyway after I completed the rest of the oral exams there. He said that would suffice. The other part of the year was to be spent on a work placement in Belgium or in French – a *stage*. This was my European Commission offer! He wanted me to stay in Northern Ireland and 'get better'. As an alternative, he offered me a research post with him over the summer months which would cover the *stage* element of my degree. Then, hopefully, I would be, in his words 'fighting fit' to start my final year in October with all my peers. So that is what happened! While I was very grateful to him for making so many compromises for me, I still felt guilty for not being able to do what I was supposed to. But I was extremely relieved to be able to finish my degree. I spent the next few months in and out of hospital and therapy. When I wasn't in hospital I was at Mum and David's but it was far from ideal. While some of my peers were working in Brussels, here I was trying to fight my demons once and for all.

Then, just when I thought things couldn't get any worse, I started to notice a few changes in Charlie. He became more distant and I sensed something was wrong. Well, I was right. It all kicked off one Saturday afternoon when he came to collect me to go out after he finished duty. You may recall as well as his normal job he was a part-time soldier. The minute he walked through the door I knew there was something wrong. He looked really serious and as if he was about to burst into tears. He asked me if we could go out as he needed to talk to me. Oh-oh, that is always a sign of something ominous. Well we parked up in a car park nearby. He didn't want to go anywhere public obviously, flip it was worse than I thought. My stomach was in turmoil. And then he said it: he didn't know if he could continue with me 'like that'! He wanted us to have a two week break so he could think things over; no contact at all. He said he had been through it all with me and he didn't think he could do it any longer. It was either him or my illness. Thinking back there had been little signs, but I had obviously ignored or misread them. I just felt sick. I wanted to die – I couldn't go on without him. I thought I was going to collapse. But he was really strong: he didn't shed a tear and said he would see me in two weeks. And with that he drove off, leaving me heartbroken and in pieces.

It was an awful night. I couldn't stop crying. I was so annoyed with myself – I hated myself and my illness. Look now I had lost Charlie too. That was it – I had to break free from this before I lost anything else. This would be my turning point! If only Charlie would hang on for me and he hadn't already given up on me. Please, please. I spent the next few days constantly crying. I tried to eat more but sadly my stomach couldn't match my heartbreak and yearning to get rid of my illness and get my boyfriend back. The result was I took really sick – my body couldn't cope with my increased food consumption and I ended up in bed ill for days. Ironically I lost more weight and the thought of losing Charlie gripped me with terror. I don't know how I got through the two weeks. I kept hoping I would hear from him to make plans to see me after the deadline. But nothing. As the end of the two weeks drew near I got really excited. I started to think about what I was going to wear and that if I didn't hear from him how I was going to show up at his parents' house where he lived.

On exactly the fourteenth day, on the Saturday morning, I rang his dad and he told me Charlie was due to come home off duty at about four p.m. So that was my plan – I would make my way to his house for four o'clock and surprise him. My emotions were all over the place: I was filled with excitement at the thought of seeing him again and the hope that it would all be OK, but at the same time terrified in case he looked at me and it was all over for good. But I had to know. As I walked the long country road from the bus to his house I begged God to give me a chance to get Charlie back. I begged for the strength to get rid of this horrible illness once and for all. I promised myself and God that if he took me back, I would really try hard and put the anorexia behind me. I would have to give up her for him.

I walked into their house and chatted to his dad for a while. He was glad to see me; he knew what had happened. Just at that moment I heard Charlie's car pull into the drive, so I hid in the kitchen. I honestly thought my heart was going to leap out of my chest. This was it. My whole life could change forever in the next few minutes.

As Charlie opened the door I stepped out. I saw his face immediately and I knew it was going to be OK. His smile was so wide and he looked so genuinely happy to see me. I just threw myself at him and hugged him so tight I thought I would never let him go. It was going to be fine. We chatted for ages about everything and I promised to change my ways. Who was I trying to kid? As if it was as easy as that. But I had to try something.

He apologised for what he had done but said he felt he had to do something to see if it forced me to realise the gravity of the situation once and for all. He expressed how terrified he had been since the Belgium episode and the real danger of losing me. That night I started off by having some of his Chinese takeaway – small mouthfuls but they were baby steps. I felt so relieved and ecstatic that we were back together again.

Now I did really try for the first few weeks, but old habits die hard and my illness and that bitch were never far away. I had to try and quell the feelings of guilt from adopting such disgusting eating habits I was told.

Then in early April Charlie surprised me again. He said he wanted to speak to me and I thought that was it. But this time, it was a much different story – he proposed to me! Yippee, he loved me and didn't intend going anywhere without me ever again. We planned a Christmas Eve wedding.

FINAL YEAR

Over the next months I started to feel and look better. I continued to follow an intensive recovery programme with Dr Adams to address physical and psychological issues with increased medication to help the onset of depression too. Charlie knew I was really trying hard. I am not sure whether it was this or my relief that he was back in my life and we were getting married, but I felt quite content.

At the start of June I had another appointment with my professor to discuss my progress and agree the starting date of my research post. I ended up working for him from mid-June to the end of September, right through the summer: typical. Most of the time I travelled up and down home from Ballydunn and the odd time I stayed with my brother and his family there. All was going reasonably well. I was able to finish my third year at university and I was on track for starting my final year of my degree and get married!

I got somewhere to stay for my final year, another nice house in Portland sharing with a few lovely first years, all Christians and genuinely sweet. I had a massive room and most weekends they all went home, so I ended up staying there most weekends too. Usually Charlie would come up on Friday after work and go home late Sunday night or even early Monday morning and go straight to his work. However, he was still a part-time soldier and the weekends he was on duty he couldn't come up, obviously. I just stayed on my own; the days of going back to Mum and David's all the time had long gone. Too much had happened; I needed my own space with my own routines. But I fretted without Charlie; I didn't just miss him, it was more panic and fearful reminders of what life would be like without him. The insecurities of my past were never very far away!

I studied really hard the whole year. I felt that I needed to prove to myself and others that I was worthy of this degree after all the trouble I had caused my university professors the previous years. So my unstinting work ethic continued and I still never set foot in the university bar. When I wasn't studying I was spending my time with Charlie or visiting Mum. When it came to the Finals I worked every minute possible. I couldn't fail. I couldn't let everyone down again.

And that was it – it was all over! I had finished my university degree and was awarded my Bachelor of Arts with Honours degree in European Business Studies with French! I couldn't believe it – I had done it. Graduation Day was 1 July, my dad's birthday, and all the family came in out in force. There I was in my gown and mortar board! One of my brothers even flew in from Canada just to be there. They were all so proud of me. It was a very special day. But guess who was there too? Yip, the bitch. My illness was still around despite all efforts. And she had to make her presence felt. While we all celebrated in a local hotel after the graduation ceremony I couldn't bring myself to go into the restaurant and dine with my own family. And Charlie stayed with me; looking back I do feel guilty for his sake but I just couldn't bring myself to eat in front of all my closest family. I just couldn't bring myself to do it even on such a special day.

Throughout my final year, as I never went out, didn't drink and ate very little, I was actually able to pay for most of our wedding with my student grant. Says it all! At the same time Charlie was saving a small deposit as we needed to find somewhere to live together.

Over the summer months, while I enjoyed having finished university, I started some of the preparations for our wedding. We also bought a sweet little country house in the rural town of Ballyrea; about ten minutes in the car from Mum. It was all getting rather exciting. I was run ragged sorting everything, but that kept my illness happy! The weight never went on.

I wasn't really thinking of work at that stage. Dr Adams had advised me to take a long break after my four years of studying and just focus on my health, our wedding and the new house. That would be quite enough. I agreed and settled on looking more seriously for work in the New Year, when I would be a married woman.

WEDDING BELLS

The lead up to the wedding was quite stressful, probably just like it is for most up-and-coming married couples. Whilst everyone was running around getting ready for Christmas I was preparing to get wed on Christmas Eve. All my family had flown over from Scotland, and Canada and a bus load travelled from Ballydunn. In fact it was the first time my whole family had ever been together – over the years there was usually one of us missing for some reason or another. It was going to be a real knees-up.

Again, like most major events in my life I went along with it all on autopilot. I wasn't worrying about the finer details of whether the cars would arrive or if the cake had the right number of tiers – my biggest fear and cause for concern was – yes, you guessed it – whether I would look fat in my wedding dress and how I could eat my wedding meal in front of so many people when obviously all eyes would be on me as the blushing bride!

Yip, I'm afraid, even on this extra-special day I couldn't escape the usual mental torture. My friend had invited herself to the wedding so she would be there to keep me in check. Not even on this special occasion could I be allowed to relax and enjoy myself. Sad, very sad!

The fact that my dad was attending the wedding and give me away in the same presence of my mum and David did give me some cause for concern. And I did feel somewhat sorry for him sitting in the far corner of the reception away from them, and a mere shadow of his former self.

But the day went fine. It was such a surreal occasion and everyone was so ecstatically happy. I was married – wow! The rest of the family partied away and had a good ol' sing-song on the way back to Ballydunn in the bus. Bless them. Mind you, they had crates of bottles of beer and but not one bottle-opener so it was a dryer journey than they had hoped but it didn't dampen their spirits!

On Boxing Day my husband and I (lol) flew off to Paris on honeymoon. Quite a place to be at any time of course but, over the New Year, the celebrations were even more monumental as the 1 January 1993 spelled the start of the so-called Single Market. The 'barriers' were to be no more and the four freedoms were to be established: the free movement of goods and services, people and money. I wondered if it was time I had my freedom too. Our honeymoon went well and Paris was superb. Plus I was able to use my French! But of course my demons came with me and interfered with what could have been the perfect start to married life...

MARRIED LIFE

Charlie and I were quite happy at the start, I think. He was working all the time juggling his day job as a store man and by night and often weekends in his role as a part-time soldier. At the start of our married life I still hadn't found employment so while Charlie was working all hours I was at home a lot on my own. Not a good thing, especially for someone with anorexia and depression. The consequences were significant: I had too much time to think, exercise and worry. And the vicious circle spiralled... my illness dominated my every minute yet again.

To give you an idea of how things were and how obviously family members worried about me, I am sharing a poem which one of my brothers wrote for my twenty-fifth birthday:

> *Hi there Ali, "how are you today?"*
> *A popular expression that a lot of us would say*
> *No honest answer expected, it's just being polite*
> *Though we really do care, be it day or night*
>
> *T'was a long time ago, that you moved away*
> *Bound for Clough, where you had to stay*
> *You were quite young, only ten if I'm right*
> *A complete new world, with not a friend in sight*
>
> *Charlie Primary was next. Where you done very well*

Made some new friends, things were going really swell
You passed your exams, and made us all proud
You were no longer, alone in a crowd

Then Victoria College was next port of call
You grew up so quick and also so tall
You worked very hard, right from the start
Like everything you do, it comes from the heart

Exams came again, but no problems there
And for the boy next door, you found time to spare
Good friends you became, I was pleased at that
And eventually settled in a Portland flat

We seen more of you then, which was really good
And we talked together, whenever we could
But a growing problem, got worse by the day
And it broke my heart, to see you this way

Where you found the strength, I do not know
By now your torment, was starting to show
Something had to be done, and a lot was tried
But all was in vain, oh often I cried

Professional help was required, it had to be
So off to the Royal, Claire Adams to see
Decisions were made, though they did not please
Prayers were answered, the chance of some ease

Graduation day was, on the first of July
We all gathered together, to watch you walk by

The Acheson Clan, with you as the star
Completely summed up, how wonderful you are

Your biggest day yet, had still to come
Charlie was chosen, the lucky one
But your health didn't change, I pray it will yet
Please help yourself Ali, your life's now in debt

Now on Christmas Eve wedding, unheard-of before
Was an ideal date, for one you adore
Sunshine at Christmas, imagine that if you can
And I felt so proud to be the best man

We went for a meal, in the White Gables Hotel
Everything went smooth, you were both looking well
There you stayed the night, in the honeymoon suite
To wake up together, what a Christmas treat

Off to Paris you went, for your honeymoon leave
Where you both slept in on New Year's Eve
The reason for that, I do not know
Your week now over, you both had to go

Well settled now, and getting on your feet
With a lovely home, 14 on the Street
Still occasional walks, in Erin town
Ali you are my, "Star of County Down"

It's the sixteenth verse now, and nearing an end
I've said quite a lot, hope I didn't offend
You're very special to me – in every way
I love you dear Ali, Happy Birthday

Your Loving brother xxx

When Charlie wasn't there I missed him and when he was late or I didn't hear from him when I should have I feared something dreadful had happened. I started to suffer from extreme panic attacks. Remember we had already been in a fatal car accident amongst other things. But what was worse, at that time we were still in the depths of the Troubles in Northern Ireland. So I had extreme genuine fear for his life. The UDR soldiers and police in Northern Ireland (known then as the Royal Ulster Constabulary but now in times of so-called peace the Police Service of Northern Ireland), lived under extremely dangerous threats to their lives and that of their families. Being shot or blown up was a real risk. After a while we heard Charlie had become a target for the IRA and so he was assigned a personal protection weapon – a gun – and bulletproof vest; both of which he had to carry on him at all times. We both had to be trained in checking our cars for the detection of car bombs before we would get in and what to do if we were threatened at home. Life took on an added level of stress and practical challenges.

One day I was in the kitchen and I heard a shot. I naturally feared the worse. Running upstairs into the bedroom in the direction of the noise I felt sick scared of what I might find. But there was Charlie sitting on the floor alone – he had shot himself in the leg while cleaning his gun! Bad enough, but could have been worse!
I started working in the public sector in 1993 so at least I had more of a 'normal' life and wasn't stuck in the house on my own. I suppose I was rather disappointed that I was not able to find employment using more directly the skills

and particularly my French from my honours degree. However, at the same time, I probably wouldn't have been very confident to deliver on this anyway. So, I was accepting of my position and work life over the following years was fine. But I once again put on the facade; my bitch of a friend came to work with me of course but continued to use her invisible cloak. I continued to attend weekly appointments with Dr Adams and I was on a variety of medication to keep me going. My weight over the years had very slowly increased to a more healthy level, as had been the 'agreed' plan with Dr Adams. However, with this departure from the 'danger zone' my friend was far from happy. She continued to berate me and make me feel like a failure. So the battle intensified and the depression set in. It was like a see-saw. As the weight went up the mood went down! There was never a balance.

A significant event happened around 1994; I started menstruating again. And to many, including, my husband, this should be seen as a good development and something to be welcomed. Up to then I had been advised I may probably never be able to bear children although that was never very much in my head. However, for me, this was horrific. I had not experienced periods for about eighteen years. In my disturbed mental state, this signified I had put on so much weight that I was now fat enough to get pregnant. I had failed – I was no longer good at anorexia – my friend was livid with me. I cried sore for days and I sunk to new levels of depression.

Sadly, Dr Adams strongly recommended admission to a mental health unit on the outskirts of Belfast called St Patrick's. Now that was its new name; it was previously called Garthill with a reputation of housing really mentally ill people. But despite the new branding to try to get away from the stigma that was Garthill, it was still referred to as that!

Now my stay there was awful – it achieved nothing positive at all. On the contrary, I witnessed too many things I wish I hadn't. As with my stay in Windsor House, because there is no dedicated eating disorder unit patients suffering from anorexia are treated in the same wards as other mentally ill patients. And although my admission to Garthill was about six or seven years after Windsor House it felt very archaic in comparison. Things certainly had not improved. Again I decided I did not want any visitors other than Charlie. I didn't want my nearest and dearest seeing me in a place like that. It was also quite dangerous as some of the patients were high risk and on a few occasions the wards had to be locked down as they were a danger to themselves and others.

After about a month of that I had had enough. My demons and I discharged ourselves. Dr Adams understood and we picked up our intensive psychological outpatient treatment immediately again. Eventually after increased medication and intensive therapy I crawled out of the darkest depths of depression and was able to function again.

I was delighted to get home. I picked up where I left off as if I had never been anywhere. It was all like a horrible nightmare but sadly I knew it had been real. I often describe my life battling anorexia as living hell!

By this stage, our married life was just OK. We had been through a lot together and obviously the strain of my illness did not help. One good thing was our travels. As we had no children and both had reasonably well-paid jobs we could afford to travel a lot. And not your normal Spain or Ibiza! No, no, no we travelled to the likes of the Caribbean, Australia, Hawaii and Bali to name but a few of our many exotic destinations. Yes, they were interesting, fun times.

However, at the start of July 1999, very unexpectedly, a few weeks before we were due to head off to Thailand, I found out I was pregnant. Yip, the Immaculate Conception – well almost! A massive surprise to everyone especially me. Charlie and I felt immediately ecstatic. It was something we had never discussed as we thought it could never happen. But the immediate problem was that I had received vaccinations for our imminent travels which I should not have done had I known I was pregnant. I made an appointment to see my GP first thing the next morning to check everything was OK. And that is when things started taking a weird turn: my doctor confirmed my pregnancy with hormone levels in the urine but when she performed an internal scan nothing could be detected. I was not completely aware of the consequence of this as I had never really been baby-cognisant! My GP arranged an urgent appointment for me in the antenatal unit of the Royal Victoria Hospital, Northern Ireland's landmark hospital, later that afternoon. I quickly contacted Charlie and explained the situation to him. He left work, picked me up at home and we headed to the Royal. The medical staff there saw me at once and started taking various tests and scans. After a few hours they advised I could leave for a break and come back later that afternoon when all the blood test results would be back. So off we went. We did a few things in town and collected our Thai *Baht* for our holidays. I felt fine and off we headed, back to the Royal.

But as we walked up the corridor the doctor and nurse who had cared for me earlier were standing waiting for me. And then it all happened so suddenly... they quickly told me I had an ectopic pregnancy and was at serious risk. I had to undergo immediate surgery. They quickly prepared me and explained that, depending on what they found, they may need to perform a hysterectomy! What, my mind was in turmoil, how could this be?

When I came round Charlie was sitting by my side. The nurses came and checked the usual observations. The consultant pulled a chair to the bedside and explained everything. The foetus had started to grow in one of my fallopian tubes instead of in my uterus, which was extremely dangerous both for the growing baby and me. This is why the hormone levels present in my body kept showing high and increasing levels indicating pregnancy but nothing was showing up in the scans. The surgery involved removing the foetus and ensuring no further damage had been done. They had to monitor me for twenty-four hours to check it had been a complete success. On top of all that we were due to fly to Thailand three days later and we discussed the matter with the consultant. At that stage he said we might have to cancel until he could guarantee I was out of danger; flying with an ectopic pregnancy could be fatal. Imagine if I had never discovered I was pregnant and had gone on holiday; the consultant explained the extreme risk I would have been under. Unfortunately the hormone levels did not come down as quickly as we all hoped. We were advised to seriously consider what our options were. Our flights were on Monday morning so realistically we had to make a decision on Sunday at the latest. By Sunday morning my hormone levels and signs of infection started to drop significantly; the consultant was content for me to go home with some medication and medical advice I had to follow. He wrote me a discharge letter which covered me with our travel insurance should anything 'go wrong'. . The decision was ours now. Would we stay or would we go? We talked it through, advantages and disadvantages, the lot and eventually we said we would go!

Once we had got that decision out of the way we talked about what had just happened. The last week had been full of every emotion possible – from finding out we were going to be parents to losing a potential son or daughter and all that went on in between! We cried.

We headed off on holiday on Monday morning and we paid to upgrade our long-haul advice under medical advice. I'm glad we did because I hemorrhaged quite badly during the flight and the increased comfort and space from the business class was badly needed. But something else was different. We had been hit by the baby bug and we knew that we now wanted to try again. We had become much closer through this loss and the future looked different in many ways. It was the first real time I think I challenged my illness head on. I was scared I would never have the experience of motherhood now and I knew my illness was a real challenge to that. My mental state was very fragile and I felt both physically and emotionally vulnerable. We tried to enjoy our holiday as much as possible and I told myself I would sort it all out, once and for all, when we got back home.

Of course I had to see Dr Adams upon my return and update her with all that had happened in the last five weeks. I had informed her the minute I learnt I was pregnant – she was as shocked as I – but I hadn't been able to update her myself on the minutiae although I knew the consultant had sent her a letter.

Dr Adams kept me under close scrutiny for the next few months as she realised the mental damage I had suffered. She also knew the psychological turmoil I was now in trying to battle my anorexia head on.

Over the next year I had two miscarriages and the stress of it all on top of my fight against my bitch of a friend was taking its toll on me and our marriage.

Unfortunately around this time my dad was also extremely ill. For the last few years my dad had been in and out of hospital and care homes in the Portlouth area. He never had a home of his own since Mum and I left. He had lived with that woman Jill for a few years until she died a couple of years back. Sometimes he stayed with his sister, my Aunt Winnie, who still lived in my granny and grandad Acheson's house in Portlouth. But she kept too close an eye on my dad and he couldn't come and go as he pleased with his drunken cronies. So with no other option he preferred to reside in a residential home. Since the wedding my contact with my dad had increased probably because I felt sorry for him and out of my guilt that I wasn't being the perfect daughter! So I would have visited him as regularly as possible wherever he was. He hadn't kept good health really since his heart attack when I was a wee girl. Plus he had years of being an alcoholic and the damage that had done to his body and mind. He suffered from chronic obstructive pulmonary disease, known as COPD, amongst other things; basically his heart and lungs were in a sorry state.

He deteriorated quite quickly in the end and the family was given twenty-four hours several times over. As Jack still lived nearby and I was living in Ballyrea at the time, albeit sixty miles away, we shared the round-the-clock vigil with Dad. I used to work by day in Belfast then drive to sit by my dad's bedside most of the night and then back home to start it all over again the following day. I did this for about six months. During that time my other brothers and sister travelled back and forward from Scotland and Canada a few times to be with Dad. It was hard seeing him so ill but on top of that was the emotional issues that his imminent passing was bringing to the fore. When he was in an angry mood he would rant about Mum and David and say horrible things which brought me right back to my childhood memories. But then I would feel riddled with guilt and fear of losing him.

It was an extremely stressful time. Of course my usual coping mechanisms kicked in and I used to go without food for days. I was basically running on adrenalin.

Then one Friday night after work I made the usual journey to sit with Dad. His feet had been really swollen with all the fluids so I bought him the cutest 'I love my Dad' slippers which would stretch for him. I also took him doughnuts which he loved. He was in terrible form that night and very ill. Then he came round slightly and demanded alcohol. I told him I couldn't get him drink; he was too ill and alcohol wasn't allowed anyway. If anything had happened Dad and he had been found with alcohol in his system I could never have forgiven myself. Well, he wasn't pleased with me to put it mildly. He started shouting and calling me lots of non-complimentary names. I got really upset and this annoyed him even more. In the end, because he wasn't getting what he wanted, throwing his slippers at me, he gave one final outburst, "F*** off then, you wee bitch!"

And that was it; I couldn't hold back my tears any more and I left...

Those were the last words my dad ever said to me. I got the call a few days later to say he had passed away. And not one of us was with him! That was eighteen years ago and I have never really got over it...

With everything that had gone on over the last few years there was considerable strain on our marriage. I had become a bit more sociable and wanted to go out with friends, perhaps to a club or to the cinema. However Charlie was tired from working all the time and couldn't be bothered. He just wanted to stay at home. His obsession was cars – vintage cars. We bought a vintage red MG midget. It was his pride and joy. In fact, I often joked it would be around long after I would... and not a truer word was said. Our marriage started breaking down. We grew apart and, under significant distress and heartbreak, I left our marital home in early 2001.

WHEN HARRY MET…

A few months later I was out with a friend for a quiet drink (well Diet Coke for me, I was driving) in town one Friday night and we bumped into a few guys. They were very friendly and we just started chatting. One of them was a guy called Harry; a tall, lean, handsome-looking guy although not my usual type. I noticed his hair was slightly grey at the sides but it suited him. I reckoned he was in his late twenties. Due to the noise in the bar we had to stand quite close to each other to hear and I happened to turn my face into his ear when we both got an electric shock. A sign – there were sparks between us! And that was it! History as they say. We talked for ages, he was recently divorced due to 'irreconcilable differences'. They had two kids: Amy and Andrew. He was living with his dad and was out with a few work friends that night. We chatted about our own personal circumstances and debated on 'what love really was'; deep and meaningful stuff for a Friday night in Belfast. Anyway, I was getting tired and felt it was time to go. Harry and I exchanged mobile numbers and he asked if he could call me some time and perhaps we could grab lunch and see how we were getting along? I said sure. However, he couldn't wait; he rang before I had even got to my car and we talked into the small hours of the morning. He was smitten for sure!

The next few weeks were like a whirlwind – we both fell madly in love very quickly! We met up every minute we could; we chatted about everything and anything and before long we were talking about moving in together and our long future ahead. It was awesome; I felt genuinely in love and excited. I was swept along by the romance and special gestures Harry made for me. This was true love; I didn't ever think I could have felt like this and Harry said the same.

Now of course, I didn't mention my illness – no way. I wasn't going to spoil a good thing. Harry did comment on my svelte physique but, like I normally do even now, I just say I lead a very healthy lifestyle. I even did the unspeakable; I forced myself to eat things I never would just to try to 'seem normal' to Harry. I had my first taste of spaghetti bolognese and curries… yuk! I desperately wanted to impress him of course. Deep down I was finding it extremely hard; I was fighting back against my illness and my old friend – needless to say she was not a happy bunny! Harry was a serious threat to her existence. I internalised all the feelings and tried to get through as best I could. My mind was tortured. I was desperately trying to seize this opportunity to start a new chapter in my life; one without anorexia. Could it possibly be? I was a little hopeful for a while…

We moved into a new apartment together and life was really good. Harry would go and see his kids and take them away several times every week. We agreed I would not meet them for a while until we felt the time was right for everybody. So I used the time when he was away to go to the gym and get all my exercise in. At least that kept my friend happy for a bit and helped my stress levels.

A few months later my divorce came through. I sorted all the necessary paperwork out and I had to arrange with my then 'ex-husband' to return to our house to remove any final belongings of mine. I was dreading that. It was planned that I would go to the house on the

Saturday when Charlie was away working so I could have the place to myself and we wouldn't run into each other. The day arrived and Harry headed in one direction to take his kids out and I headed the other direction to my old home.

I had been so swept up by the events of the last few months that I hadn't allowed myself to think in the slightest of what I had come through and what I was leaving behind. I wasn't prepared for how I was going to feel when I went through the front door. I was immediately met by familiar aromas and sights of memorable furnishings. I was overwhelmed by emotions and burst into tears. I think the emotions of the last year just caught up with me and I couldn't control myself. I got hysterical at one point and just sat on the floor and cried. I felt so alone and for the first time since I had met Harry, I asked myself what I was doing. What had I done? Was I doing the right thing jumping into another serious relationship so soon? I realised, like many events in my life, I was being carried away by the doing without allowing the thinking. It took me quite some time to work my way around the house, room by room. Each time I opened another door memories came flooding in and I couldn't stop them. Before I knew it, hours had passed by and Harry had been trying me on my mobile. As I hadn't answered him he started to panic. He told me afterwards that he started to worry I was having second thoughts and perhaps Charlie had been there and persuaded me to give them another go. I'm glad he hadn't been in the house because I was too upset to deal with his emotions on top of my own. I knew deep down Charlie wouldn't have been there that day anyway. While he had been quite romantic during our relationship he was quite stubborn as well; he never stood up and fought for me. If he had maybe we wouldn't have been in that situation. No, I knew he wouldn't dare appear on the Saturday when he knew I was to be there. He would wait until the Sunday night, after his weekend shift was over, and then come home to deal with his own emotions knowing I had been and gone for the last time.

It was sad.

When I arrived back at the apartment it was about seven-ish. Harry was waiting for me; very relieved to see me walk through the door. After giving me the almightiest of hugs he handed me a small card. He had written how much he loved me and he had even pricked his finger and put a drop of his blood on it. It was a sign of his true love for me, straight from his heart; I still have it in my purse to this day. It was all going to work out, I reassured myself.

The next few months were good although my old habits were creeping in again. I continued to see Dr Adams and took the usual medication. I had told Harry a bit about my illness but not the full glorious detail; best not! I wanted to give us a chance; not chase him away at the first hurdle when he realised there were three of us in this relationship!

THE LEAVING

All this time I assumed Harry was happy too. We both worked hard; he was in the private sector and I the public. He continued to see his kids regularly and I did my own thing when he wasn't around. When we could, we went out for walks, to the cinema and to clubs. We both loved dancing. Every so often Harry would get calls from his ex-wife about the kids and he would have to go and sort something or other. He was a good dad.

Then one day I started to take chest pains and went to see my GP. I was diagnosed with inflamed muscles around my heart due to stress and I was signed off work for a few weeks. So I was hanging around for a few days in the apartment when suddenly, one afternoon, Harry arrived home in the middle of the day in a state. I was resting in bed, under strict doctor's orders, and he asked me to come into the lounge as he needed to talk to me. Uh-Oh! I quickly looked into the driveway and I couldn't see Harry's car. I was confused; I just didn't know what was happening. By this stage Harry was sitting on the couch and then he said it, 'It's over.' 'We are over'... At first, I thought I was hearing things. He couldn't have said that. No, it couldn't be over. What about our *Castles in the sky*, one of our favourite songs in the charts at that time, we often said was symbolic of our dreams together. I was begging him not to go. I felt desperate. I felt sick. The familiar feelings of heartbreak and abandonment were overwhelming. He tried to explain that he had to go back to his kids. It wasn't that he didn't love me but he loved his kids more. How could I argue with that?

That was Tuesday and Harry said he would leave on the Saturday morning. He had it all sorted. I suddenly felt utterly betrayed and stupid. I had no idea how he had felt all this time and obviously this had been in his head for a while. Immediately my usual coping mechanisms kicked in – I started being sick and I didn't even want to look at food. I had to be punished. Obviously I had done something seriously wrong that Harry couldn't love me enough to stay with me. I had given up everything for him and now he was leaving me. I didn't want to go on. I was at a disturbingly low ebb. It was a good thing I was off work on sick leave because I couldn't have gone into the office; I could barely function. I spent the next few days numb, dragging myself from the bed to the couch, crying constantly. At the same time, Harry would come and go, where to I wasn't sure but I guessed. Then when he was at the apartment he would go outside every so often to make phone calls, again I'm not sure to whom. I felt he just couldn't wait to get rid of me and go back to his wee family. He sat and openly told me all the plans; he was going down that Thursday night to talk things through with his ex-wife and discuss the next steps. I remember seeing him shower and dress that night in the knowledge he was going back to the family house. I felt so ill in every way.

Saturday morning arrived and I lay in bed not wanting to get up as Harry moved about the apartment like a whirlwind, packing up his belongings. It was real, he was going. Then after an extremely tearful goodbye, he was gone! I felt sick; I had lost the love of my life. I didn't want to live any more. I knew I had to contact Dr

Adams urgently. She increased my medication and put me on a daily contact programme. She was genuinely worried about me as were my family; well, the ones I had told. I felt so stupid. My family hadn't even met Harry and now I had to tell them he had left me. My insecurity levels were at an all-time high. I felt worthless. At times like this my illness stepped in. And not to support me but instead to kick me when I was already down.

    I couldn't settle myself that night knowing Harry was back at his marital home and would be so happy to be surrounded by his kids and maybe even his wife. I didn't know what to think any more, I thought I knew him but I obviously didn't. I started to question all our time together; was everything he had told me just been lies?

    The next morning I woke and suddenly felt sick when I remembered I was all alone. Then my phone rang and it was Harry. I couldn't quite believe it. He asked how I was and he told me he felt rotten for what he had done and he missed me. We rang each other several times over the next few days and eventually we agreed to meet the following weekend. He said he would come to the apartment. When he walked through the door we stood and looked at each other for a split second, then we ran and hugged as if we would never be separated again. We talked over everything that had happened and how we both were feeling. He regretted what he had done but he said he couldn't leave the kids again. We were both distraught. We didn't know how it was going to turn out but at least he still loved me. I mustn't be that awful after all, I tried to tell myself. But my friend immediately started telling me to make sure and keep him this time; that it was my fault he left me in the first place!

As the weeks passed by Harry and I were in regular contact. We gradually built up a normal relationship again except this was far from 'normal' and we were not living together. But I was mentally scarred by what he had done to me and I wasn't sure I could ever fully trust him again. But I did love him and felt I couldn't live without him. However, I was so mentally unstable. Furthermore, I really resented how I felt so desperate and unloved and I hated what I had become – the other woman! He came and went from the apartment as it suited him and left me alone to return to his family. I felt dirty and horrible. I had to be punished. As you can imagine, I could always rely on my good ol' coping mechanisms to get me through. So I ate less, exercised more and the weight fell off. Well, I had to do something to make me feel good about myself.

HARRY'S DAD

And just when things were stable or as stable as such an abnormal situation could be, there was another blow!

Harry's dad, a young healthy man in his early fifties started to feel unwell. Harry took him to hospital for tests and sadly he was diagnosed with an inoperable brain tumour. Naturally, the family was devastated. It was such a shock too that it was hard to accept. Harry rang me immediately from the hospital once he had heard the news. I felt distraught for him. But what could I do? Right there, right then I had to see Harry; for his sake and mine.

I had never met any of his family before and this wasn't exactly the time for introductions. While this news was horrific enough, and certainly not being selfish, I knew this would have major implications for me and my already vulnerable state of mind.

As I was still the other woman I couldn't be seen. I couldn't publicly be there for Harry. I couldn't attend the wake or the funeral. It reiterated the dirty role I felt I was playing in his life. So I jumped in the car and drove to the hospital car park. I found his car and parked beside it. At some point he had to return to his car. I sent him a quick text message to tell him I was there. After about ten minutes there he appeared barely able to walk. He got into my car and I held him. He just burst into tears. We sat there for a while and he composed himself. He said all the family was meeting at his sister's house within the next hour and they would start making the necessary arrangements. He had to go. I was left feeling like a 'bit on the side'; unwanted and unloved. I turned to my usual habits to keep me company.

The next few months were awful. I continued to live in the apartment on my own. I had gone back to work at this stage but I was very unstable. I was living in this renewed state of insecurity and vulnerability. I really felt as if I was living 'on my nerves' as the old saying goes. Harry would call to me most evenings and I would have a clean shirt for him to put on before he would go to see his dad in the hospital, and later, the hospice. His dinner would be ready for him; I was desperate to please him in every way for fear he would leave me completely again. He wasn't staying with me; after hospital he would head back to the marital home – happy families had to be played faced with the adversity of what was going on with his dad, he said. In fact, he often intimated that if "anyone" were to put any sort of pressure on them he would not appreciate it. So, I stayed on my own every night aware that Harry was sleeping miles away in their former home. Not easy, I can assure you. My physical and mental conditions were bearing the brunt of my personal predicament.

Then in the middle of November 2001 there was another turn of events. Wait for it; I had a funny feeling I was pregnant! I never said anything to anyone, not even Harry. I was really worried how he would react in light of everything going on. He was still calling to the apartment when he could and we were in regular contact by phone. We had ordered new furniture for the apartment months ago before he had left me and, strangely enough, now that we were back together 'in a sense' the furniture was only now being delivered. So we decided to take a day off work and spend it together in the apartment awaiting our new furniture. While we lay there watching television on the couch I suddenly started bleeding really heavily. Harry guessed immediately; he had heard me being sick that morning. We both panicked. We reckoned I had probably been pregnant and miscarried. He drove me at once to the chemist for a pregnancy test and I rang my GP. The test came back positive; oh my goodness, I was pregnant. However, my GP gave me an appointment first thing the next morning to examine me; there was the possibility I had miscarried and the pregnancy hormone was still in my body, thereby giving me a positive pregnancy reading. I had to get confirmation one way or the other as soon as possible. Harry left shortly afterwards to go to see his dad, who had now been moved to the hospice to spend his last days; he had been given a few weeks to live by this stage. I spent a very surreal night alone wondering what the hell mess I was in! I didn't know if I was pregnant or not. I didn't know whether I wanted to be pregnant or not. And I didn't know if I had a long-term partner or not! What a fine mess you got me into, in the words of Laurel and Hardy. Well I sure as hell deserved any punishment coming my way, I heard my bitch of a friend say. It turned out I was pregnant and had suffered a threatened miscarriage.

In my initial weeks of pregnancy I was extremely ill, couldn't eat a thing hardly – which only 'fed' (no pun intended) my eating disorder but not great for the baby. Furthermore, I had threatened miscarriages every few days. I was in and out of hospital regularly. Now that the shock of the pregnancy had sunk in I was ecstatic so I was living in the added fear that I might lose the baby. Needless to say I was off work. Sadly, I was going through a lot of this on my own; Harry was still living away and I was only getting the chance to see him when he could fit me in between his other commitments to work, his dad and his kids. I felt as if I was his last priority and in fact deep down I felt as if he was annoyed with me for getting pregnant! None of this helped my insecurity issues, for sure.

By now I had taken the bull by the horns and told my family about the baby. The news was certainly not what they expected to hear from me. Again, I felt as if everyone thought I had let them down, that I was a disappointment to them. I had been through so much that year and had to tell them another bit of shocking news! As usual, I 'put on a face' and kept all my fears and loneliness to myself.

Christmas was looming and I was dreading it. I knew Harry would have to spend most of it with his kids; the rest of the time he would be at the hospice no doubt. I understood of course but that didn't help my feelings when I woke up to an empty house on Christmas morning. I visited my mum and David for a few hours but they had their own plans, so I headed back to the apartment late afternoon. Harry called to freshen up and see me before he headed to visit his dad. He had eaten his Christmas dinner with his ex-wife and kids. I never had any Christmas dinner; not that the dinner bit bothered me, rather the opposite. It was more what it signified. I felt like nothing more than a bit of dirt; unwanted and unloved. What a mess I was in, and I knew I had to get my act together for my baby's sake but it was extremely hard. On top of that I didn't have my normal medication and antidepressants to help me through. The minute I found out I was pregnant I decided to stop everything. I wanted to do the best for my baby.

Sadly, Harry's dad died on 29 December. Obviously I was gutted for Harry but I was there for him as much as I could be behind the scenes. It was me who accompanied Harry to buy a new suit for his dad to wear. It was me who went with Harry to the funeral parlour to see his dad and make the funeral arrangements. It was me who comforted Harry when he cried at nights. But it wasn't me who attended the funeral. That was his ex-wife. His ex-wife stood by his side at the graveside. It was his ex-wife's name in the newspaper *Memoriam* alongside his. I didn't exist in Harry's other life. It hurt. It hurt big-style. I just couldn't settle myself to think it would ever work out and I would have a partner to help raise our child. I was at a low ebb. I took myself to the cinema on the day of the funeral; it was too much to try to deal with at home on my own.

After his dad's funeral Harry spent a few nights with me our apartment. It was great; I felt grateful that I wasn't alone and he was there – how desperate is that! At least we brought the New Year in together; he just made it to be with me before the clock struck. I hoped that was a good sign that the next year would be a good one: 2001 had been my '*annus horribilis*'. Well another one.

THE WAITING GAME

January brought its own issues. I had a date for our first scan but Harry couldn't be there, it was another poignant time for me when I saw our child's long legs. A footballer in the making, the midwife said to me! But I had no one to share in that experience. Harry started to spend more and more time with me at the apartment, staying over some nights at the start and then the odd weekend. Obviously I was pleased; he must love and want me after all. But that brought constant arguments and phone calls all the time from his ex-wife and her family and friends. Eventually, at the end of January Harry decided to move out of his marital home once and for all and move back to me. He had his reasons for leaving in the very first place; the second time was because of me and our baby-to-be. While I was naturally relieved to have him back, I also felt guilty for him leaving the kids again. Furthermore, I was still so insecure that I didn't trust him enough that he would stay forever. He had shattered my heart once how could I be assured that he wouldn't do it again.

When I was much younger and throughout my illness, I never thought I would have kids. For a few reasons I think but one of them was the obvious; the fear of getting big, yes big and fat. You see, unlike nowadays or as other normal people view it, I could not see past the big bump. I was not able to appreciate the beautiful glowing woman carrying their offspring and so it never really occurred to me that motherhood would ever happen to me. As fate would have it my body didn't either as, coincidentally or really as a consequence of the illness and loss of weight, my periods stopped in my mid-teens and never resumed for many years. So during all that time having children never really entered my head – it just wasn't an option.

So when I did become pregnant, although not in the ideal fairy tale way, which I have told you about, I was ecstatic; but scared.

The first weeks and months of the pregnancy were extremely traumatic as I nearly miscarried on several occasions. At least now Harry was with me at night and able to accompany me to the hospital appointments and scans. We also started antenatal classes. It was still all a bit surreal for me and I must admit I was getting quite anxious about the pending birth and motherhood. How would I deal with having a baby and my eating disorder? It was then that I began to really struggle with my illness and the battle got very hot and heavy. But this time I had to think of someone else – my baby. So when I knowingly went without food or questioned my activities I had to really stop and think about what I was doing to my baby. I never wanted to hurt my baby and I knew by living out my illness in my usual way and listening to my friend that is exactly what I would do.

The sickness and weakness was so intense in the first few months that I was told by my doctors to have bed rest and eat regularly; all bad words to an anorexic's ears. That sounded like hell, how was I to do that? But yet I knew if I didn't I would be depriving the living person inside me. It was a real struggle and one I knew I could not win without paying a price. Obviously I had to stop all my medication, another struggle. The antidepressants helped me cope with fighting against my ever powerful friend. So the months passed by and, yes, naturally I grew bigger. Our baby was thriving. I often asked myself was this not a good excuse and an opportunity to shove off the anorexic mantle once and for all and start truly living? This was it – on a plate as such – the one explanation for why you were eating, resting and taking care of yourself – because you had a baby and you needed to for their sake. It was without doubt the best excuse ever, much better than the guilt I would suffer if I just gave up the illness discarded like an old toy in a box, no longer wanted! I kept telling myself this was my chance, an opportunity to start again, not for myself but for my baby. This was the chance – and yes I often did try to look up at that sky and search for some ray of light – some light bulb moment when I would be able to say, that's it, call it a day, pack your bags you bitch. Call yourself a friend – you are out of here. Try as I might, that's not quite what happened.

I managed to get through as best I could, eating the minimum amount I could to nourish the baby and little enough to satisfy my friend. But I had to do it for my baby. I couldn't hurt my baby. I often asked myself why I could eat like that for someone else, but not myself. Why did I in my own right not deserve to be satisfyingly fed? The million dollar question to which I never got an answer. It is probably one of the hardest parts of the illness. The struggle between the two sides is much harder than one side having complete control – the fight between right and wrong brings shouting and fighting. Much easier to have peace and suffer the consequences!

The battle within me continued. My friend just wouldn't go away!

THE NEW ARRIVAL

But things did not go quite according to plan! On 12 June 2002 I went to work as usual. However, shortly afterwards I started to feel unwell. I wasn't quite sure what was wrong, I just didn't feel right. I rang Harry at work and when he asked me how often I was feeling unwell and I answered about every three minutes, I could almost hear the sharp intake of breath down the phone. Needless to say he pulled up in the car outside my work very soon after that. I couldn't be in labour, it was too soon. I assured him and myself. The baby wasn't due for another four weeks! When I arrived at the Royal Victoria Hospital maternity ward the nurse examined me and told me I was already three centimetres dilated – told you I had a high pain threshold – I was already in labour! I was given steroid injections to try to assist the baby's lungs as they were still underdeveloped and I was admitted to the antenatal ward. In fact, the staff nurse told me not to even unpack as I would probably be going down to the delivery room soon. Well, that didn't happen. Everything stopped. The contractions lessened but I was too far along for them to let me home. I had to stay there until the baby was born.

In fact, I was in that antenatal ward for two weeks until my consultant, Dr O'Brien, decided they would induce me on 25 June. I saw many women come and go and I was still there! It was a long two weeks and my bloody friend was giving me a hard time. I was being constantly monitored by the medical staff, being fed regular meals and had no privacy whatsoever. All very overwhelming on top of the fact that I was about to have a baby!

Anyway, the big day arrived and, I suppose just like every mum-to-be, I had mixed emotions; nervousness and excitement! Harry arrived to be my side and they induced me at around eight-ish. It was a very long, strange day but at two minutes after six p.m. our darling daughter, Victoria, was born! I was a Mummy! Surely that euphoric feeling was enough to say farewell to my illness for good? Some family members arrived to see the latest addition to the family! I was taken down to the maternity ward shortly afterwards and Harry kissed Mum and daughter good-night. None of us knew what lay ahead...

Not long after Harry left I started to feel ill; now what followed was very much like an out-of-body experience. I felt as if I was fainting, then losing consciousness. The next thing I knew was that a few nurses were attending me; one raised the bottom of my bed saying she was trying to let the blood go to my head, and the other was taking my blood pressure and pulse and started saying that they "were losing me"! It was all so bizarre – I could hear and see everything go on but in a distant dreamlike fashion, although this was more of a nightmare. More nurses were around me then and they had pulled the curtains around me by that stage. I heard them say to call my family immediately and page the consultant; apparently I was clotting and they needed to operate urgently. They said they didn't even have time to move me; they would have to work on me there in the ward. The next while was more of a blur as I slipped in and out of consciousness. I recall Harry arriving and I took off my oxygen mask to try to talk to him. Then two doctors arrived and I heard them say they would have to try to remove the clots by hand as they were running out of time. But suddenly someone else said they better get me to ICU as I needed urgent blood transfusions as I was losing too much blood. Then there was more blur and the next thing I recall I was in an operating theatre; there seemed to be medical staff running everywhere. I think then I thought I was dying because I asked them to bring my baby to me; they quickly brought Victoria sleeping soundly in her baby cot to my bedside. At that point I thought that was it. I was then wrapped in a silver blanket and I was being given a blood transfusion while they tried to remove the clots. Harry was in the corner just sitting, numb. Then for the first time I actually started to feel real pain; I don't think I had been given any pain relief at all as they were so busy trying to save my life. I removed my oxygen mask once again and asked for help; they quickly gave me a morphine injection and I started to fall in and out of consciousness again.

It all seemed to go on for ages and every time I opened my eyes the room just looked chaotic. It was the early hours of the morning by this stage and I realised they must have managed to remove the clots. It seemed calmer and there were fewer staff around me. I remember opening my eyes fully and Harry was sitting in a chair on my left-hand side with his head on the bed and Victoria was sleeping peacefully on my right. For a split second I didn't actually know whether I was alive or if this is what it felt like to have passed away and to be looking down on my loved ones; it really was very weird. I was still all hooked up to various monitors and wrapped in the silver blanket. After a few minutes a nurse and doctor came and spoke to me. They checked my pulse and blood pressure. I had survived!

I stayed there for a few hours and once I was stable they took me back to the ward. Harry reluctantly left to go home. The nurses tried to let me settle and maybe get some sleep. They knew what I had been through. They took Victoria into the baby room to look after her and I remember just lying there trying to absorb all that had happened. But I never got that chance; minutes later I heard a few babies crying from the baby room and even though my daughter was only hours old, I distinctively knew she was crying. I wasn't allowed out of bed so I rang my buzzer and asked the staff to bring Victoria to me and I would feed her. And that was that; I eventually had my daughter in my arms and she was beautiful. As I cuddled her I thought I was going to burst with so many emotions. I remember saying to myself that that must be it – I literally nearly died – surely this was the sign my illness had to go? I had too much to live for. Obviously someone of much greater authority thought I deserved to survive! For a split second I felt a bit of hope that my friend would set me free...

I stayed in hospital for another week and needed a few more blood transfusions before I could go home. Victoria was thriving; she was just a little darling. I still couldn't believe I was a mummy. The nutritionist visited me to chat to me about the severe blood loss I had suffered and how anaemic I was. She discussed my normal diet with me and it was then the talk of my illness came up. She was very sympathetic but stressed the importance and seriousness of my current condition particularly after "what I had been through". I was prescribed lots of medication to try to help my severe anaemia and low energy levels.

    I never really thought too much about what had happened the night after Victoria was born, or maybe I just didn't have time between looking after my baby and having loads of visitors. In fact the only time that fateful night was ever mentioned was the night before I was to be discharged. Just before my visitors were due to arrive the staff nurse who had been on duty that night called to see me. She was actually on leave and lived 70 miles away but had made the round trip to see me specifically. It was only when she started saying that she never thought I would survive that night that I was reminded of the near-death experience I had just had.

FAMILY LIFE

I couldn't wait to get home and try to start afresh with my new wee family. Looking back at the photos of me in hospital I looked deathly pale and so ill but, as usual, I couldn't see it then. To me I just looked and felt fat – you see, my illness hadn't gone; it was just waiting for me!

The next few days and weeks were hectic. I suppose the same for most new mums. I think I was still in shock about what had happened but was living in denial. I started feeling very down but everyone kept saying it was the usual postnatal blues; I didn't say to anyone that I knew it was more than that. Harry and I never mentioned what had happened; it was like the elephant in the room – we just got on with our new parenting roles.

And this is the way it was for the next few years. I was very ill for some time and Victoria was quite a sick baby with chesty issues, probably as she was born premature. She also suffered projectile vomiting and she never slept! Or rather it seemed that way. I was always exhausted. We moved to a bigger home and I returned to work; Victoria was in full-time nursery care. Life was busy and as you can imagine after having given birth my illness was very tough on me and made sure I quickly lost any pregnancy weight gained. Business as usual...

I had continued to see Dr Adams regularly and then she announced her retirement. This was a major blow for me; she had been my lifeline, literally, for years – I feared how I would cope without her. But, despite her advice that I carry on with another highly recommended psychiatrist, I decided I would try to go it alone.

After Victoria was born neither Harry nor I ever talked about having more children. Every precaution necessary was used. And any vaguely related baby comments from Harry were rather negative and suggested there definitely would be do more. I think deep down he too was haunted by the night Victoria was born although he never said as much; but he must have been – he had to sit and watch me nearly lose my life having given birth to our daughter!

After a few years Harry could take it no more. He was terrified I would get pregnant again so he visited his GP and got an appointment to have a vasectomy the following month. That was that! I recall driving him to the hospital that morning with a heavy heart. I couldn't say anything but I knew the finality to the consequences. Like many things in my life I just had to get on with it and try to stifle any real feelings. I just had to do as I was told!

And life trundled along. Victoria was growing up fast. Harry and I were fine; we had a comfortable lifestyle and holidayed to exotic places whenever we could. But my illness and my friend were still there.

Following Harry's New Year's Eve marriage proposal I said yes and we had a sunset wedding in the Maldives that March. Just the three of us: Harry, Victoria and me. It was bliss, really romantic and our darling daughter was our wee flower girl. Life would appear good.

Amy and Andrew still came to stay with us quite often and they accompanied us on various trips and family holidays together. The three kids would all fight of course, as siblings tend to do. However, Amy and Andrew openly admitted to everyone that they got double of everything because their parents were divorced! They took advantage that was for sure! Around the time Amy turned fourteen years old she became quite a handful. She started to get quite rebellious and got into a lot of trouble. Her mum threw her out of her house on a few occasions and she came and stayed with us for months on end until she decided she wanted her back. No matter what I did, no matter how good I was to Amy and Andrew, I was still seen as the wicked stepmother; and that was hard!

Then as time passed Harry and I had a change of heart and we started to talk about wanting to have another baby. I know, I hear your say, "But Harry had a vasectomy." I know. Nothing straightforward in my life, eh?

So we talked it all through and eventually we decided that we wanted to try, to give it our best shot – no pun intended. So we paid a private consultant and in November that year Harry underwent a medical procedure to try to reverse the vasectomy. Afterwards we were told the operation had been a success and there was every chance Harry was fertile once again. For the next few months we were quite loved up and we both felt extremely happy that I might get pregnant soon again. However, nothing happened and after a check-up with the consultant the following year we were told the operation had not been a success after all. We had to brave the news that we would not have any more children, well not naturally anyway!

This was devastating news especially after we had been told the opposite months previously. We had lived in vain hope. There was immediate disappointment and my usual coping mechanisms quickly stepped in to get me through. I stopped eating and my mood plummeted. So Harry and I talked again. The desire to become parents again was overwhelming we just couldn't just give up at the first hurdle. So we started looking into fertility treatment and particularly a new type called ICSI – or in full, intracytoplasmic sperm injection. ICSI differs from conventional IVF (in vitro fertilisation) in that the embryologist (doctor!) selects a single sperm to be injected directly into an egg, instead of fertilisation taking place in a dish where many sperm are placed near an egg. We gathered all our information and I arranged an appointment with my own gynaecology consultant, Dr O'Brien, to discuss the way forward.

We entered the room full of high hopes and left in despair. To cut a very long and painful story short Dr O'Brien strongly advised us against considering any form of fertility treatment. He mentioned the night of Victoria's birth and he actually opened my medical file and referred to that fateful night's events. That was the first time anyone had actually really explained what had happened to me. Dr O'Brien told us that I had suffered excessive postpartum haemorrhaging – basically part of the placenta had not been removed properly and it was left in my uterus – it caused me to clot and bleed excessively. I was lucky to have survived. Dr O'Brien went into the medical detail and said that he was not confident I would not suffer a similar experience if I was to give birth again. Furthermore, there was no guarantee I would survive another one.

I can still remember the words vividly because right there right then I felt my whole world fall apart. Harry and I were both numb and the tears silently rolled down my cheeks. Dr O'Brien was great; he explained all our options and he also gave us his expert advice; forget about having more children, do not take the risk. He appreciated our circumstances and how distraught I was. He kindly gave me his personal e-mail address and said if we still wanted to proceed with ICSI he would help us and if we wanted to contact him with any other queries, not to hesitate. We left the room different people. We sat in the hospital canteen for about an hour just crying and trying to make sense of the way ahead. We both headed back to work and tried to get through the rest of the day.

The next few days were surreal. My usual coping mechanisms stepped in and I felt as if my friend was laughing at my misfortune, as if she saw me getting pregnant and having another baby as a threat to her existence! Harry and I were really upset and we tried to talk it through, but to no avail. We were on opposite sides of the fence by then. Harry was adamant that we couldn't go ahead and had to give up any thought of another baby. He said there was absolutely no chance I could put my life at risk. End of discussion. However, me being me, I didn't agree. I felt so desperate to have another child I was prepared to chance it.

Then two nights later Harry got an urgent call to say his daughter had been rushed to hospital. He went straight over to learn she was seven months pregnant – she was fifteen! She didn't even know. The irony and pain couldn't have been worse. Here we were so desperate for another child and there she was, at fifteen, doing all sorts of things she shouldn't have been doing at her age, pregnant! It was like a sword in the heart. It made it all the more painful. I was so jealous. At one stage I started thinking we could raise the baby as ours. I was at rock bottom.

Eventually I e-mailed Dr O'Brien to say we were not proceeding with ICSI. He was very supportive and recommended I attend a fertility counsellor; he set it all up. However, Harry wouldn't go with me, he wouldn't talk about our issues. The only way he could deal with the pain was to blank it out, pretend it wasn't happening. It was so poignant; couples were supposed to attend these and there I was on my own. He wanted to deal with it in his own way regardless of how I was or what I needed. The fertility counsellor was really great and felt even more sympathetic as I was visiting her alone. But she believed my most recent depression surrounding the inability to have more kids wasn't the only problem – apart from the obvious.

In utter desperation we even considered adopting or fostering to try to meet the emptiness and hurt we were both feeling. However, after contacting several organisations and going through in depth talks about what was involved we reluctantly decided it was not the answer. That was the final door of hope closed firmly in our face.

Harry and I started to drift apart and I fell into deep depression. I started taking panic attacks and couldn't bear to see babies or even go into a shop if there was anything baby-related. I just fell to pieces. I couldn't see Amy and didn't want to hear any of her baby news. On the other hand, Harry was being Mr Practical and was taking her out shopping and preparing her for the forthcoming arrival. And of course I had to try to carry on as usual at work and at home for Victoria's sake; she couldn't know any of this! My friend was punishing me.

She made me 'keep up appearances'. I had to keep going, she said. I had to please everyone. I couldn't let anyone down. Consequently, I resorted to my inner friend to get me through...

BREAKDOWN

I basically just made it through to the Christmas break. In November our daughter, Victoria, had also been unwell and had been rushed to hospital following a bronchial/asthmatic attack which certainly did not ease the pressure but, thankfully she pulled through admirably. Harry and I really needed, and were depending on, the Christmas leave period to try together to face the surrounding issues and get some badly needed physical and mental respite. However, during the Christmas break there were a number of further setbacks. Victoria took ill again on Christmas Eve and my aunt died suddenly. The stress was overpowering. Not the most relaxing of Christmases but obviously we got on with it for Victoria's sake. And on top of that, Amy was due to have her baby any day. I was dreading it.

Our granddaughter Penny was born on New Year's Eve. I was full of mixed emotions. Feeling desperate I had to see her immediately. I felt like a crazed woman. When I saw her and cradled this beautiful tiny bundle in my arms I thought my heart would break. This was the baby I so badly longed for. Why should this young teenager have an unwanted pregnancy and me be denied a baby? Life was cruel. Instead of becoming a mum again I had just become a nanny! I went home and cried myself to sleep – Happy New Year, eh? The following morning we awoke to the news my six-month-old baby cousin had been found dead on New Year's Day. I just about got through the next few days, numb from one emotion to another – I felt under extreme pressure. On the way home from the baby's funeral my body basically 'crashed' and I started showing extreme physical and psychological symptoms of stress overload. I took a mental breakdown. It had all just become too much for me; the baby's coffin was so symbolic. I spoke to my GP the next morning and after seeing me she immediately signed me off work on sick leave indefinitely. She also prescribed me various medications to address the sleep, depression and panic attacks. I was a mess. In then end I was off work for over two years.

I never saw Penny again until she was nine months' old. I just couldn't; the pain was too much. As usual, when I couldn't deal with something I just pretended it wasn't happening. Yes, denial, that is the answer. If I didn't see her then maybe she didn't exist. Instead, I resorted to my usual old habits to get me through this latest heartbreak. But it wasn't easy. Obviously Harry wanted to spend time with his granddaughter and Victoria her niece. So when they went to visit and take Penny out, I stayed at home and exercised excessively.

By this stage my fertility counsellor was extremely concerned by my mental state so she referred me to a perinatal depression and trauma psychiatrist in the Royal Victoria Hospital, Dr Donnelly. She was of the opinion I was still suffering post-traumatic stress disorder from the ectopic pregnancy, subsequent miscarriages and my near-death when Victoria was born. I underwent some intensive treatment with her and was then discharged back to my local mental health unit.

There I saw a counsellor on a weekly basis and I had emergency contacts should I need help 24/7. My counsellor was great but knew she couldn't really help me. I knew that too. But she wanted to try something. She referred me to the eating disorder service outpatient service based in Loughshore Hospital in Antrim, another hospital in Northern Ireland renowned for treating mentally ill patients. I had various tests carried out to assess my physical condition; it was suspected that most of my internal organs had shrunk following years of malnutrition and starvation – they were most likely working at full capacity. I also had a DEXA scan; this is a special type of X-ray carried out to measure bone density. I was diagnosed with osteopenia, the pre stage to having osteoporosis!

Referral to Loughshore was quite a milestone and not a good one. This was the first time I had been to eating disorder counselling since Dr Adams retired several years previously. I felt as my life was going round in circles and I couldn't get out. I was starting to feel that utter helplessness again. What was I doing? I was a grown woman, I had to take control of my life again. I desperately needed to get rid of this illness once and for all.

However after a few weeks of this latest round of treatment I had had enough. I was really annoyed with myself for agreeing to more help and I felt it was like a backward step. My friend was raging with me. So I said I would not be back. I had to sort this out myself once and for all. I told my GP that I no longer wanted to waste their resources. Let's face it, there was nothing they were going to tell me that I didn't already know! I could write a book – oh funny, I am!

Unfortunately, while I was off on sick leave I did not get the opportunity to fully focus on my illness or rather the intensive treatment for, and potential recovery from, it. My mum took ill and, after months of debilitation and being treated for various things, she was rushed to hospital one afternoon very ill and later diagnosed with a hernia. The hernia had gone undiagnosed for some time. All the symptoms had been there for several months but she had been misdiagnosed. She had been given an injection for a frozen shoulder after complaining of pains in that area; all along it had been down to the hernia. The hernia was so large it had pushed Mum's stomach and internal organs up into the top of her chest. It was the hernia that was causing the stomach pains, nausea, pains in her shoulder and general sickness all along. Anyway, once diagnosed she had to undergo emergency surgery whereby they removed the hernia and stapled her organs back down where they belonged. Mum was in hospital for quite a while and afterwards came to me to convalesce. Obviously Mum required a lot of attention while in, and after, hospital. So needless to say, she became a high priority for me during that time. I am delighted to say that she came through it and we have just celebrated her eighty-sixth birthday!

Not long after we got Mum on the road to recovery, we learnt my brother in Canada, Robert had throat cancer. Naturally, we were all devastated although we never told Mum. There was no point in upsetting her unnecessarily. She still does not know to this day. It was another worrying few months between operations, skin grafts and follow-up treatment. But again, he pulled through and has just enjoyed his sixty-sixth!

And while all this was going on there was another major issue. Amy, sixteen at that time, was getting wild again only this time she was a mum and had Penny to look after. Her mum threw her out of the house again. She went AWOL for a while and we had to contact the Police and Social Services because we didn't know where she or Penny were. It was an extremely stressful time. Once we had found her it was agreed that her, Penny and the current boyfriend in tow (not Penny's dad) would come and live with us until we got them a house. After months of being at ours, which was absolutely chaotic, we got Amy a council apartment. We paid for everything she needed to start up a new home, from curtains to carpet and beds to bowls. We did everything we could to make them comfortable in their new wee home. Needless to say, this all created additional stress and work for Harry and me. But I bore the brunt as I was there at home all day supposedly 'with nothing to do'. Furthermore, Penny had got used to me being around, and actually started to call me Mummy – it was me who looked after her when they lived with us and even after Amy moved onto her own home, her priorities were throwing a house-warming party and having mates around. I ended up looking after Penny for long weekends. At least I knew she was safe then; I worried about her 24/7. Naturally, with my illness and my history regarding my inability to have any more kids this was a double-edged sword. Penny was my heaven and my hell all wrapped up in one!

To do something really nice for Amy and Penny, Harry and I decided to treat everyone and take Amy, current boyfriend, Chris, Andrew and us to Disneyworld, Orlando Florida for two weeks at Christmas. Taking into account all the flights, villa with swimming pool, park tickets to all the Disney and Universal parks and spending money it cost us approximately £12,000. But we thought it would be a super treat for them all. It should have been but it wasn't! Amy was her typical selfish, arrogant self the whole time. But it culminated on Christmas Eve; she caused a massive argument with Victoria around the most spectacular Christmas Tree having just watched the marvellous Macy's Christmas Parade. It was absolutely awful; she was a real bitch, a disgrace! Amy called Harry and I all the names of the day and accused us of all sorts of things. She said she had just come along to spoil the trip for everyone. Well, she succeeded. Christmas Day was one of the worst ever but Harry and I did our best for Andrew, Victoria and Penny. We just about got through the rest of the holiday for the sake of them. I couldn't wait to get home – what should have been the holiday of a lifetime had been turned selfishly into the holiday from Hell.

Harry and I were relieved to get home but there followed months of nasty texts and calls from Amy. It was a really difficult time for us. We didn't get to see Penny for ages. Things eventually settled down and contact resumed, as usual, when Amy needed us to look after Penny or money. She was predictable.

So much for my time off work to get myself better!

And guess how I got through all this added stress? You are right – instead of being off work to try to 'get better' and fight my illness I ended up relying on my coping methods to get me through all the other stressors in my life. Maybe it was all fate – my friend didn't want me getting rid of her so maybe she was secretly sniggering!

I decided to go back to work. Against medical advice I started back to work in June 2013: new job, new people, new start. It was all going to be fine, I kept telling myself. No one would know me or my history. Maybe I wouldn't need to put on such a front; maybe I could be more of my real self? Was this another chance to get rid of my ol' friend? To try to support me I reluctantly agreed with my specialists that I would attend the psychotherapy unit of another local hospital. I said I would give it a go.

TRIAL AND ERROR

Not long after this another major event in our lives happened – yes, another one!

Harry was accused of very serious bullying and harassment allegations at work. Nonsense of course. He was an easy target for others to try to cover up something wider. He was an innocent victim. The immediate impact on him was extremely worrying. Now I will not go into all the detail but suffice to say the shock and absurdity of the things he was being accused of made him extremely ill and he suffered a mental breakdown a few weeks later. I sadly witnessed firsthand how my husband was affected by it all. Prior to August 2013, I would have said my husband was a highly reliable, conscientious IT professional who worked long hours to deliver the highest quality of service to his employers. He is, as I would often call him, an 'IT geek'; he was an expert in his field, excelled in his job and was very much a team player. He had been involved in very high-profile projects and had proven to be a highly professional and valuable member of the senior management team.

Right from the outset of the case all our time was consumed by the allegations and in-depth drafting of responses and audit trails. Harry very quickly became a shadow of his former self: only ever talking about the investigation, little or no interaction with anyone including our daughter, showing signs of shaking and had trouble eating and sleeping. He continued to be extremely withdrawn and was in deep depression. Panic attacks and extreme anxiety verging on paranoia were the norm. He often unintentionally frightened our daughter by his behaviour and our married life was practically non-existent. I became his mere counsellor and carer. The only real conversations we had were about the investigations and our days and often nights were spent going through more evidence and drafting reports.

This all went on for approximately two years. Under legal advice from a good friend we got a lawyer and barrister and took our own case of disability discrimination against Harry's employer due to how he had been treated. After years of fighting we won; his employer settled out of court just before the trial was to start. That part of it was over! Harry is better than he was but still not like his former self and I fear things will never return to the way things were. I was his support throughout and you know who was mine! Yip, you know by now how I coped – my friend was there by my side.

Now I must admit I found it hard being there for Harry the way I did because he hadn't been there for me. But he needed his wife by his side and I didn't let him down. I did everything in my power to support him. Until he experienced mental illness he never appreciated what I had gone through in my darkest depths. But worst of all, he never tried. He understands that now.

I had made it. I had got through this last difficult chapter in an all too eventful life with anorexia by my side. Friend or foe? The next day I started writing this book. Since then I have had further treatment for both physical and psychological effects of my illness; it was only a matter of time before things started going wrong again…

That was a few years ago now and, needless to say, there has since been many a drama in my ever-eventful life. But I am coping as best I can...

So there you have it. That is my story... certainly not a pretty one and not an easy one to read, but it is real life, my real life, nothing made up or exaggerated. In fact I have spared you a few dramas. I am sure you all have your own thoughts; maybe it is disgust, pity, sympathy, disbelief. And sadly for some of you there are maybe a lot of similarities, maybe not in the events of my life story but in the thoughts and behaviourisms that have dominated your life, too? If that is the case, please take comfort that you are not alone, I understand what you are going through.

WHERE AM I NOW?

Hi there! My name is Alison North, usually just called Ali.

I am a mother, a wife, a daughter, a sister, an aunt, a nanny, a cousin, a friend, a neighbour, an employee… and wait for it… a genuinely decent person!

I continue to strive for perfection in my work just as much as my home life. My friends and colleagues often tease me about how much I do! My personal life is dominated by looking after my husband and our daughter. My mother is still alive and well and I care for her too as often as possible. I try to keep in regular contact and do what I can to help my siblings who are still located in various corners of the globe. I keep myself busy 24/7 whether at home or away. Aside from my duties as a mother and wife I exercise and walk somewhat excessively. I garden and do housework to extreme OCD levels. I cut the edge of my back and front gardens with kitchen scissors. Yes you heard, kitchen scissors, much to the amusement of our friendly neighbours. And now I have started to write! I am constantly busy; I have to be! I eat little, but enough to get through. But I am still here to tell the tale, as they say… still fighting…

REGRETS?

Now looking back I often ask myself, do I regret my life? Do I wish it could have been different? What would I have done differently if I hadn't lived a life battling anorexia?

Firstly and most obviously, of course I have regrets. I am extremely saddened by how my life has been dominated by this illness and this bitch! I wish I had never started and continued my secret friendship with anorexia! I wish I had got rid of her a long time ago. You see, I have had to experience many things I would rather not have. I wish I could have spared my family and loved ones the horrendous worry and heartache that came along the way. But that is the way it is. That was me and the person I have been for the most part of my life. Fate moves in the strangest of ways, you cannot always see it at the time but it does. If my life had been different I may not have crossed the paths of some of the many wonderful people along the way. I would not be where I am now and that is hard to feel remorse for!

WHAT NEXT FOR ME?

So what is next for me, who really knows? But what I do know is I am more determined than ever that this illness, this so-called friend has controlled and destroyed my life for thirty years now and that is it. I have had enough. She cannot take any more from me, I can't let her. The friendship is over; my dirty, guilty secret is out in the open. I cannot play this life-threatening game any longer. The bitch is packing her bags and I am throwing her out! It is time to start living my life for real and let the torture come to an end. I have a lot of living to make up for. Now I know it will be tough and there will be hard days but I will do this; I have to. I have come too far to give up now. I have lots of other true friends…

PART II

WHY ME?

So why me? Why is my life like this? Why me and not the girl in front of me in the queue or the girl next door? Well, I have asked myself that very question hundreds of times over the past thirty years and you may be surprised to hear, the answer is not "just because"! It is me for a reason and it is others, like me, for similar reasons. Read on …

The medical science behind this illness is mind-blowing and the various techniques used to treat patients vary greatly across the world and over time. But let's start with some basics…

WHAT IS AN EATING DISORDER?

Eating disorders are a form of mental illness defined by abnormal eating habits that negatively affect a person's physical and mental health. There are different types of eating disorders – anorexia nervosa, bulimia nervosa and binge eating disorder being the more commonly known ones. Sadly, anxiety disorders, depression, and alcohol or substance abuse are common among people with eating disorders as they find the eating disorder itself unbearable to suffer.

A recent report by PricewaterhouseCoopers states over 725,000 men and women in the UK, of all ages and backgrounds, are affected by eating disorders.

Furthermore, although eating disorders tend to be associated with females, 15-20% of sufferers are boys and men.

But it is important to stress that, although serious, eating disorders are treatable conditions and full recovery is possible. The sooner someone gets the treatment they need, the more likely they are to make a full recovery.

Eating disorders are more talked about today than ever for various reasons. Firstly, more people, mainly females, suffer from an eating disorder; and secondly, it is more widely reported! The media and society in general tend to portray the thin body as the ideal figure. Models strive to be thinner and weigh less than one another; look at the birth of size zero. This influences society and some try to change their eating habits so they too can look like that and be as popular or as envied as the magazine pin-ups. Many try different slimming methods, one after the other, and this often plants the seed for an eating disorder. Furthermore, modern lifestyles and the insane increase in gadgetry and online technology means people do not need to move about as much – even the shopping can be delivered without you moving from your chair. You do not need to leave the house to visit friends or family, sure you can ring or Skype them or tell the world and their granny what you are doing using Facebook or Instagram! But sadly, that couch potato attitude brings a more couch potato body because even though fewer calories are being burned off that does not mean fewer calories are being consumed! And while sport and exercise are an essential part of any healthy lifestyle the media can encourage an unhealthy focus on body size and weight and set unrealistic targets for the body.

In fact, legislation came into force on 1 October 2017 in France in an effort to fight against the problem of anorexia where it is reported about 600,000 people suffer from anorexia or another form of eating disorder. The new law forces publishers to disclose if an image has been digitally doctored to make the model look thinner than they actually are.

ANOREXIA NERVOSA

In this book I have been talking about anorexia nervosa, or just anorexia, as this is the illness from which I have suffered.

Approximately 10% of those diagnosed with an eating disorder suffers from anorexia nervosa. With this illness anorexics try to keep their body weight unnaturally and often unhealthily low by dieting, using laxatives or excessively exercising.

The term anorexia nervosa actually comes from the Latin meaning "nervous loss of appetite". This definition sums up the total lack of understanding about the disease. It is not that sufferers of anorexia nervosa do not have a lack of appetite, they do! But they are terrified of gaining weight and so they restrict their eating and try to tell themselves they are not hungry and forbid themselves to succumb to their ravenous hunger. Obviously anorexics are individuals and thereby their personal traits may differ from one person to the next. However there are extremely distinguishing and common behaviourisms. People with anorexia see themselves as overweight, even when they are dangerously underweight. Anorexics typically weigh themselves repeatedly, severely restrict the amount of food they eat, and often only eat very small quantities of certain foods.

Untreated or even treated, anorexia can last for many years. For some it will always remain with the sufferer. While it may become more manageable, for some it may never go away – the sufferer just learns to live with it! Previous studies have found that, with the appropriate treatment and support, almost half of anorexics make a full recovery. Unfortunately, approximately 20% remain chronically ill.

Sadly anorexia has the highest mortality rate of all mental disorders. While many young women and men with this disorder die from complications associated with starvation, others die of suicide. The inner battle against the illness often becomes too much. A recent report states that 50-75% of sufferers with anorexia also have depression. In women, suicide is much more common in those with anorexia than with most other mental disorders.

However, it is very hard to obtain accurate figures as those who suffer from an eating disorder may ultimately die of heart failure, organ failure, malnutrition or suicide. Often, the medical cause of death is recorded instead of the eating disorder that caused the subsequent ill-health.

HISTORY OF THE DEADLY DISEASE

Eating disorders have existed for a long time and have been written about throughout the world. Historical evidence suggests that anorexia and bulimia have been around since the first century. During the time of Caesar, wealthy Romans would overindulge at lavish banquets and then try to make themselves feel better by vomiting so they could return to the feast and eat more. Throughout history, a form of anorexia has been customary in different religions with people fasting for days in preparation for getting a sacred message from God. Many religions today still practice fasting for a certain amount of time to show their devotion to their lord.

Although psychologists and other behavioural scientists have known of anorexia for some time, the general public first got to know about the illness towards the end of the twentieth century. It was in the 1970s, that the American media began to write about anorexia and they featured stories about how young women refused to eat, but without really explaining how serious the illness could be. The disease continued on the increase and was often considered to be a disorder amongst young rich, white girls.

The first real 'celebrity' death related to anorexia was Karen Anne Carpenter. Karen was born in 1950 and with her brother, Richard, formed the 1970s duo The Carpenters. She was a very talented musician. Not only was she a skilled drummer but she had an amazing voice. Karen suffered from anorexia, of which little was known at the time. Although she seemed to be on the verge of recovery sadly she died at the age thirty-two from heart failure caused by complications related to her illness. Her death led to increased visibility and awareness of eating disorders.

Since then many celebrities have opened up about suffering from an eating disorder or other form of mental illness. One well-known female icon described it as a 'horrible, paralysing' disease which "robs you of living your life." Never a truer word!

Today sufferers of eating disorders can be anywhere and everywhere – the normal girl or guy in the street and celebrities alike. No one is safe from this type of mental illness.

WHY DOES SOMEONE DEVELOP ANOREXIA NERVOSA ?

There is no simple answer. If only there was. While there has been a lot of research into the causes of eating disorders there is no exact explanation. Eating disorders arise from a combination of personal, family, physical or genetic factors as well as life experiences that may cause someone to be both emotionally vulnerable and sensitive about their weight and shape. Dieting has a role to play in the development of an eating disorder, in fact in most sufferers the eating disorder grew out of dieting behaviour. But it does not mean that if you diet you will go on to develop an eating disorder.

While professional views of anorexia may differ, they do teach us something about the inner world of someone with this condition – or the person most likely to get it. The illness is associated with people of low self-esteem, problems coping with the uncertainty or problems in life and managing relationships with other people.

A comparison of the psychological profiles of those with anorexia found these prevalent factors: perfectionism, high self-expectations, competitiveness, hyperactivity, repetitive exercise routines, tendency toward depression, body image distortion and obsessions with dieting and weight. The anorexic personality yearns for a simple uncomplicated life, free of pain and loved by all.

HELP AVAILABLE

As you can imagine help for eating disorders is inconsistent at best and varies from one town or country to another. However, it is improving, albeit slowly. Basically, there are those treatments to help the physical problems and those to try and address the mental issues.

Physical Treatment

Sometimes GPs are not formally trained to understand or treat eating disorders, although their help in managing physical risk can be invaluable. Most National Health Service trusts only provide a service for the most serious cases of anorexia and, due to demand, there may be long waiting lists or only help in non-specialist mental health units. Under certain conditions, where an individual's eating problems have led to physical or emotional crisis, a more intensive approach is often needed such as being in hospital or in a more structured treatment programme. You may be able to access these services through your GP or directly through a private hospital treatment service. The fees for private inpatient or day care treatment are likely to be very expensive but may be funded in some cases by private health insurance.

Even at the onset of my illness treatment for anorexia was focused on the physical. It seemed the answer was simple! Eat more, gain weight, there you go, problem solved! Now, why didn't I think of that?

This continues to be the predominant form of treatment used to 'shake some sense' into the majority of sufferers either as outpatients or inpatients. In my time patients would be fed high-fat, high-calorie diets, possibly even force fed if thought necessary. They would have been put on bed rest with physical activities severely restricted. So naturally the end result over time would be weight gain but at the cost of the patient's mental wellbeing. Not only does this torture the mind but visibly the patient feels themselves growing before their very own eyes. Furthermore, their stomachs would have shrunk through months, maybe years of eating little so it is physically impossible to start eating considerably larger amounts of food on a regular basis without your body reacting in the form of nausea, diarrhea and general feeling of illness.

Linked to these various harsh treatments are the prescription drugs, which would range from various kinds of antidepressants, relaxants and possibly sedatives. When I was in hospital the drugs round dished out quite a party mix sometimes. Thirty years on I still take quite a concoction of medication daily.

PSYCHIATRIC TREATMENT

Now that is not to say the only treatment available for those suffering from anorexia was aimed at the physical; that is not the case.

As I have already told you, from the outset of my illness in my teens, after referral from a hospital physician I had been attending, I was hospitalised; put on bed rest and force fed for two weeks – that is when I came under the magnificent care of Dr Adams and there began a long relationship lasting almost twenty-five years! Throughout all my time as an out-patient under Dr Adam's care I saw her in various offices linked to different mental health units throughout the Belfast area. Dr Adams treated me with an intensive psychiatric therapy programme in tandem with a physical one. As I described earlier in my story, I saw her regularly and she basically kept me alive.

THERAPIES

A form of therapy called **Cognitive Behavioural Therapy** adapted for eating disorders is sometimes recommended. CBT, as it is often known, is a "talking therapy" that can help you manage your problems by trying to change the way you think and behave. Unlike some other talking treatments, CBT focuses on the now; it looks at your problems in day-to-day life, rather than going through issues from your past. It tries to show you more logical, practical ways to improve your state of mind on a daily basis. It is often used to treat anxiety and depression but can be used for other mental and physical health problems.

Now to the most recent therapy I received which is **schema therapy.** At the start I thought, here goes, another cracker attempt to brainwash the mentally ill – but I was pleasantly surprised and you don't often get to say that with this illness. But I can honestly say throughout my thirty years this most recent 'therapy' has been the most life-changing for me!

SCHEMA THERAPY

What is it?

Schema therapy is one of the more recent types of psychotherapy used to treat patients suffering from various forms of mental illness. It was developed by Dr Jeffrey Young, an American psychologist. If you want to learn more on this yourself you could try some of the books and articles I have read; they are included in my bibliography at the end of this book. However, I will try to explain some of the key elements of schema therapy and how I have been able to learn from it.

How Schema therapy works

In Dr Young's work on schema therapy he talks about people's behavioural types called "schemas" or "modes". For instance, the *Child Modes* which, as the name suggests, describes the different ways a child typically feels or behaves.

In normal life if a child is upset or is faced with having to deal with difficult situations they quickly learn how to cope. However, children learn to cope in different ways depending on their behavioural type.

As Dr Young explains, the *Compliant Surrenderer* child copes with life in a passive, approval-seeking way around others out of fear of confrontation or rejection. They tolerate verbal and/or physical abuse scared of the consequences. Consequently, they are unable to express their own basic healthy needs or desires to others for fear of negative consequences familiar from their past experiences. I identify strongly with this mode – maybe you do too. The *Detached Protector* ignores or suppresses their own basic needs and feelings. They often live in a state of numbness or detachment in order to protect themselves from what they fear is to come or the unknown in general. This is how they cope with life's challenges. They would often pursue distractions or physical activities in a compulsive way or to excess to avoid conflict or close relationships with others for fear of consequences experienced in their past. I can definitely relate to this mode too!

However, while these ways of coping helped the child at that particular time or for a particular incident when they were young, using the same coping mechanisms in adulthood is not healthy. For an adult to deal with life and the challenges it brings by behaving the same as in childhood is extremely unhealthy and, unfortunately for many, extremely dangerous. But sadly that is all the 'child' knows; that is the only way they know how to cope. So that is where the battle begins. The 'child' has to fight against what up to now has been their norm, their safety net, their all.

Throughout this book, as part of my illness I have often spoken about 'voices' inside my head or the other part of me telling me off or being nasty to me. In schema therapy language this is explained. Dr Young refers to them as *Maladaptive Parent Modes* – maladaptive meaning 'not adjusting appropriately to the situation'. Doesn't exactly roll off the tongue, does it?

In adulthood, someone using the *Punitive Parent* (one of the Maladaptive Parent Modes) coping mechanism constantly feels guilty of doing wrong and believes they should be harshly punished even for simply existing. They often act on these feelings by being extremely cruel or abusive towards themselves. There is no room for human error or imperfection. Dr Young explains that when someone tries to deal with life using the *Demanding or Critical Parent* (another Maladaptive Parent Mode) they believe and behave in a way that, at all costs, they must strive for perfection and put others' needs before their own. They think that it is wrong to express their feelings. In fact, they become angry at themselves for having or showing needs. They do things to punish themselves, such as cutting or starving themselves, for instance through eating disorders. These individuals think of themselves in an extremely critical way.

Basically these types of coping mechanisms used in adulthood can explain what is happening when you take on or 'hear' the voice of a parent or similar abusive adult from your past. You internalise the shouting and demanding behaviour that that adult showed you as a child. It is the punitive and/or demanding parent you hear. So you talk to yourself as if you were them. You punish and criticise yourself as they punished and criticised you in the past. And your healthy-adult side is you trying to answer back and stand up for yourself for what you truly and properly deserve. So this is where the two sides come in. The good and the bad, the healthy and the unhealthy – the parent against the child!

This is the battle. Instead of fighting back it is often easier for the 'child' to let the louder voice win and 'surrender' to the critical, punitive parent! And this is how the mental illness strengthens and deepens until you feel hopeless as if there is no way out. You are a small, helpless child again.

How Could Schema Therapy help you?

I do not want to repeat what the professional books say nor bog you down in heavy terminology or medical science. Instead I want to tell you in user-friendly language how schema therapy has helped me and more importantly, how I think it could benefit you or others in similar positions facing similar problems.

Schema therapy can help you understand why you behave in certain ways and gives practical, realistic advice about how you could change. Now it does not solve everything. You do not read the book and that's it and you can run about eating and drinking and being merry without a care in the world – as if! I am afraid it doesn't perform instant miracles.

But what it does do – is help. It helps you to understand the why? It helps you understand that because in the past you did this and, because you behaved like that, it is all you know. So it tells you quite firmly that you need to fight back – you need to question and challenge why you should still continue to feel, think, behave and respond in the same way as you did as a small frightened child. It gets you to ask yourself, what is the worst that can happen... if? It encourages you to ask yourself, what if I did this? what would be the consequences? It makes you think. It makes you challenge everything but in a healthy way. It provides hope that the future does not have to be like the past or the present – it provides hope of a new future, a new chance to lead a full life without fear of consequences. For me, that means hope for a new life without suffering constant fear of eating or thinking or doing. A new life without dreading not being liked by everyone or fearing you are not doing enough for others all the time. A new life allowing yourself the needs, physical and emotional, that you want and deserve. It provides hope for a better future!

What Have I learnt from it?

For me I found schema therapy helped explain how previous events or stages of my life had made me the person I have been all these years to the person I am now. It has helped me understand why I do what I do; why I behave the way I behave. It helps explain how I desperately needed and wanted to find solace in something or someone. Something or somewhere I could control and feel I was safe and doing what I wanted. Sadly the only solace I could find was in my anorexia. And the irony is that it ended up controlling me.

I could literally picture, recall and sometimes relive real life events and with the help of schema therapy I gradually learned to understand how and why I dealt with particular events in the past, both as a child and as an adult. For instance, as a little girl I saw my life as trying to be there for Mum, scared to leave her in case Dad hurt her again. I had to try to please her and Dad, doing anything possible to save the situation or make them happy with me at least, if not with each other! And when Mum and I had to flee and live our new life I pretended my life was different; I made up a family and I made up where I lived. I was desperate to be accepted as part of the gang, I tried to be someone I thought others would want to be with. I was really continuing my role as a people-pleaser, being compliant with everyone at all times. Looking back this type of behaviour are classic signs of *Compliant Surrender Child Mode*. And I am still like this today! I try to do everything and please everyone.

And the classic signs of *Punitive and Critical Parent Modes* were evident and continue to be omnipresent in my life even today. For instance, as a young adult when it came to my education and my self-drive to attain the highest results it was only me beating myself up if I did not do well. I had become my own *Punitive Parent*. When I did not meet my high standards I called myself a failure and swore that this would never happen again – I had to study more and get into the top class. I had to punish myself. And guess what, I did – I was in the top class ever since. But at a price! I had become my own *Critical Parent* making demands upon myself and then my own *Punitive Parent* punishing myself if I felt I had failed.

    Schema therapy has taught me that how I dealt with something in the past became the only way I knew how to deal with similar situations since then and till this very day. I quickly recognised that nothing would change and my life would continue along the same rugged, painful path until I learnt and found myself capable and wanting to try to break that cycle once and for all. I finally thought there was a glimmer of hope for this to happen through schema therapy. I finally saw some flicker that all was not lost.

So I started to look at the past and break each bit down into manageable chunks. Then, once you can understand why you have learnt to carry out certain behavioural traits, you can decide to challenge certain things. You can consider, well, is that the way I should be dealing with that? What is the healthy adult ideal way of responding to that situation? In turn you can ask, what if I behaved in another way, what would happen?

Another benefit I felt from reading many of the books and articles on schema therapy was learning about other people, like me, suffering similar problems and leading similar lives. Not that I enjoyed reading about other people's problems, not at all, but it was somewhat reassuring that I was not alone. I was comforted that this is a real illness that deserves real help and real treatment; a serious disorder that we all deserve to be free of. That always makes it slightly easier. You are not alone. We are not alone. There are thousands of people out there like you and me who need help but who can change. I am one of them and so can you be!

These are only a couple of psychological therapies used to treat mental illnesses, but two which I have personally experienced.

I am glad to say there have been a lot of changes, for the better, for sufferers of anorexia and other mental illnesses, since I was young. Today, the internet and social media has its benefits. As I will point out shortly, there are real lifelines out there, at the touch of your fingertips. During my research for this book I came across a number of extremely invaluable organisations who are doing amazing work for those so desperately in need.

SELF-HELP

Complimentary to professional help, or perhaps in some cases instead of it, sufferers of eating disorders and anyone interested in learning more on this type of mental illness may benefit from some sources of self-help such as:

- **Self-help Groups:** Some people are comfortable and find benefits from talking within self-help groups, either as therapy groups or support groups, which help people to come together, find friendship and normalise their feelings around food and weight. These types of groups can help those suffering from an eating disorder as well as their families.
- **Specialised Literature**: Other forms of self-help are to be found in books, articles or CDs.
- **Internet:** there is a wide range of information available on the internet which can prove vital, from understanding symptoms of an eating disorder to sources of help. I have listed some links to extremely invaluable organisations here.

Useful Websites

- **Beat**, the UK's eating disorder charity.

    Beat's vision is an end to the pain and suffering of eating disorders. They aim to be a champion, guide and friend to anyone with an eating disorder by:
    - Challenging stigma and misunderstandings around eating disorders at every level.
    - Translating the complex and technical into practical guidance.
    - Listening to people affected so that they feel less alone with their eating disorder.

    Beat provide information and support through helplines which people can call, text or email; online support including information, message boards and online support groups; and Helpfinder, an online directory of support services.

    Beat's work is invaluable for the many sufferers who they have helped since they began in 1989. They are inspirational with their belief that recovery is possible.
    www.b-eat.co.uk

- **FightED** (fighting Eating Disorders) previously known as CARED, is a charity that supports families affected by eating disorders in Northern Ireland. It was founded by two families from

Northern Ireland, both of which had a daughter who suffered seriously from an eating disorder. FightED's mission is to provide support and advice to parents and carers who have a loved one suffering from an eating disorder.
www.fighted.org

- **MIND** is a mental health charity which provides advice and support to help anyone experiencing a mental health problem.
www.mind.org.uk

- **National Centre for Eating Disorders (NCFED)** offers a very comprehensive website which provides information on eating disorders including advice on counselling, helpful sources of further information and a contact option.
www.eating-disorders.org.uk

- **National Health Services (NHS) Choices** provides mental health helplines for anyone concerned about themselves or a loved one.
www.nhs.uk

MENTAL ILLNESS IN THE UK

A report in 2015 by the King's Fund, an independent charity working to improve health and health care in England, claimed that the mental health sector was under a huge amount of pressure. Driven by the need to reduce costs, the report cited that only 14% of patients said they had received appropriate care in a crisis.

In early 2016 THE INDEPENDENT reported that David Cameron, the then UK Prime Minister, announced a billion pounds extra investment would be ploughed into mental health services across the country, claiming more than a million additional people would receive treatment each year in England by 2021. However, sceptics pointed out such promises had been made previously. In fact, research by the BBC and the online journal Community Care, in March 2015, showed that budgets for mental health trusts in England had fallen by more than 8% in real terms between 2010/11 and 2014/15. In monetary terms, this was equivalent to almost £600 million. Figures from the NHS's health and social care information centre, showed that the number of qualified nurses working in psychiatry dropped by 10.8% from 41,320 in 2010 to 36,870 in 2015.

On 9 January 2017 the UK Prime Minister, Theresa May, announced plans to try to change attitudes to mental health, with a focus on children and young people. While the Prime Minister's announcements were very welcome there was still some scepticism. The mental health charity

Mind said while it was important that mental health issues were being raised at that level the evidence would be improved services and support for those suffering from mental illnesses.

At that time, Government statistics said one in four people will suffer from a mental disorder at some point in their life, with over half of mental health problems starting by the age of fourteen and 75% by eighteen.

It has been widely recognised for some time that mental health has played the poor relation to physical health. And eating disorders are only one of the many types of mental illnesses suffering from this disregard.

As part of the reforms, by 2021, no child would be sent away from their local area to receive treatment for mental health issues. This is welcome news for those patients who have had to travel long distances for treatment due to bed shortages. A case was recently reported of how a nineteen-year-old girl from Buckinghamshire had to be treated in a specialist eating disorder unit for her anorexia in Glasgow, nearly 400 miles away from her family home.

At present more than 1.6 million people in the UK are estimated to be directly affected by eating disorders. And figures are on the increase; statistics from NHS Digital show that there were 2,913 hospital admissions for eating disorders in England in 2015/16 compared to 2,287 in 2011/12.

The increasing number of stories in the news about sufferers of eating disorders highlights that this deadly disease can affect all corners of the globe and from all walks of life. It can hit old and young, black or white, celebrities and Joe Public alike.

Newsreader Mark Austin recently revealed his teenage daughter, Maddy, had suffered from anorexia and depression. Sadly, the two often go hand in hand. As many anorexics will agree, having an eating disorder is like having a ticking time bomb in your head 24/7.

The ITV News journalist said that even when his daughter had lost four stone and was close to organ failure they were unable to get the right help. He said she needed urgent treatment but was instead offered counselling once a fortnight. Fortunately, Mr Austin's daughter is reported to be doing well thanks largely to their ability to access private funding. In a very recent personal television documentary entitled, *Wasting Away: The Truth About Anorexia* Mr Austin and Maddy spoke of their experiences and stressed the devastating impact eating disorders can have on the victim and their families. In the documentary HRH Prince William spoke about his hopes for more awareness and openness about mental health. During the nineties Prince William's mother, Diana Princess of Wales, very courageously spoke publicly of her battle against an eating disorder. Furthermore, HRH Prince Harry raised the profile of mental illness when he recently opened up about his own mental health issues following the death of his Mum.

Hopefully the increased media and disclosure of personal experiences from all walks of life can serve to highlight the desperate need for increased awareness, support and funding for mental health including eating disorders throughout the UK.

THE STORY IN NORTHERN IRELAND

And in Northern Ireland, a small part of the UK often overlooked when it comes to key service delivery, the situation is far from ideal.

In October 2015 the BELFAST TELEGRAPH reported that the then Northern Ireland Health Minister Simon Hamilton announced he had asked his department to examine if a specialist unit could be opened in Northern Ireland. In 2013, 307 adults and 109 young people were treated for eating disorders in Northern Ireland, and ten were sent to England for treatment.

Since there is no specialist facility for treating eating disorders in Northern Ireland, inpatient treatment for adults is carried out in general hospitals. Children who require inpatient treatment are usually admitted to the Beechcroft mental health unit, on the outskirts of Belfast. It is Northern Ireland's only inpatient facility to treat children with mental health problems. However, treatment there has been heavily criticised.

The horrendous story has recently been made public of how a GP in Northern Ireland told the parents of an eleven-year-old girl with an eating disorder to simply take her home and get her to eat, showing no sympathy or comprehension of the illness. The parents said that after they began noticing some behavioural issues around food, they took the girl to see a GP in December 2013. After the GP tried to examine her, the GP printed out a body mass index graph and told them to take their daughter home and eat, and the GP would see them again in three months.

This incident was disclosed as the health watchdog published a review into the standards of eating disorder services in Northern Ireland. The Regulation and Quality Improvement Authority (RQIA), the independent body that regulates and inspects the quality and availability of Northern Ireland's health and social care services, reported significant issues and made 11 recommendations to improve services.

Among the issues highlighted by the RQIA was a lack of awareness, support and communication from GPs and others in the medical profession. Adult patients and carers complained that finding out more about eating disorders was difficult, with many sourcing information from the internet.

In the twenty-first century this should not have to be the case! These sufferers should receive the most effective treatment from the outset. Just like cancer or any other potentially life-threatening illness, the earlier an eating disorder is treated the greater the chances of recovery.

In June 2017 there was good news for the people in Northern Ireland. According to media reports, as part of a financial deal following an agreement between Northern Ireland's Democratic Unionist Party and the Conservative government, there will be an extra £50 million towards mental health provision. Very welcome news!

Now that is not to say there are not some invaluable sources of help in Northern Ireland; I can vouch for that. Throughout my illness I have received immense support and treatment from various medical and psychological professionals. But unfortunately, resources for mental health and, in turn, eating disorders are just too stretched.

In Northern Ireland fightED (fighting Eating Disorders) is a charity which has been set up by two families, both of which had a daughter who suffered seriously from an eating disorder. Due to the lack of adequate services or facilities in Northern Ireland, they had to fight to have their daughters treated by specialist units in London, where they eventually made a full recovery. Their personal experiences inspired them to set up the charity in order to support, educate and empower other families affected by eating disorders. They offer support and practical tips for sufferers and their families. As part of their support services they offer New Maudsley Model workshops, designed to help carers cope with the trauma a family experiences when an eating disorder affects a loved one. While this help has been available to families in mainland UK for over twenty years, it was not available to Northern Ireland families. Thanks to fightED this invaluable course has been available since September 2014, so far helping hundreds of families.

FightED strongly believes that it is unacceptable that the most ill and most vulnerable patients have to be sent out of their own country in order to access the necessary treatment.

Eating disorders affect around 20,000 people in Northern Ireland, yet for many it is still an illness covered in shame.

THE FUTURE

So what does the future hold for people like me, you and all those other families out there impacted by anorexia? Well, it is likely that cases of anorexia nervosa will continue to rise as they have been doing since cases first started being recorded.

The only good news is that anorexia is not the hidden or forbidden condition it once was. There is much more information about the illness, symptoms, its causes and potential treatment – one major benefit of social technology and information at your fingertips!

Furthermore, supply and demand is starting to kick in with the increase worldwide of more dedicated treatment services, a growing range of therapies and dedicated eating disorder specialists who not only try to help those currently suffering, but help research efforts that will hopefully help or even prevent future sufferers! I can only pray that areas like Northern Ireland will get the specialised eating disorder unit it so desperately needs. Today, we know more about the disease and how deadly it can be! So hopefully this will help other innocent victims like me, maybe you or someone you love.

WHAT NEXT FOR YOU?

If you are reading this as a fellow anorexic, I beg of you to listen to my advice. If you are reading this as a relative or a friend of someone suffering, or you think may be showing early signs of anorexia please talk to them. And if you are reading this simply as someone who wants to learn more about this subject, well, then I thank you. The more people know even a little about this potentially killer disease the more chance there is of sufferers getting more support and treatment to fight back.

MY ADVICE?

Don't go down this road!

Don't get into that relationship with anorexia nervosa – it is a relationship that in many ways may kill you. Stop striving for the imperfection you think will give you that happiness, security and love you yearn for. It won't! Don't be fooled that you will ever feel happy with yourself – you won't! No matter if you weigh five stone, six, seven or eight stone, you will never be happy, you will always feel you could, and you should, lose more weight – that's the illness with you in its grasp! Eating less actually tricks your body into thinking you need less to survive so what in effect happens is your metabolism slows way down. So while you may lose weight even to a seriously dangerous level for some time eventually, from even eating the littlest amount more, you will start to gain weight. Stop striving for perfection: you will never be happy. You will never ever believe you are perfect even though you are! So don't get into that trap – it is one that anorexia will never let you win!

Be honest with yourself and others!

The first thing to do is admit there is a problem and for others to be aware and open too. It is not always about what an anorexic eats, albeit that is the visual clue; it is more about how they think and feel about what they eat and what they fear are the consequences of doing so. Just because someone eats little and healthily it does not necessarily mean they have an eating disorder. If they see their food as a basic need and a normal part of life, that is great, no problem there.

It is when someone eats little and purposely denies themselves anything else even though they feel so hungry they could eat forever and they have headaches and dizzy spells and will not allow themselves another bite until they have walked for hours or exercised excessively. Or when someone thinks they are disgustingly fat and are too embarrassed to eat in front of others as they think they will look greedy weighing in at a low weight – now there's someone one with severe anorexia. See the difference? The inherent problem lies in the mind but is openly manifested in the body!

Recovery is about re-educating the brain about proper eating habits and the need for them. It is about stopping the mind from playing tricks. So before the mind is able to get total grasp and control you need to be able to answer back: that is the only way you can overcome this torture. It is a battle but it is one you can win!

This is where the two sides come in – the good side and bad side, the good twin and evil twin, or whatever you want to call them. And the battle commences: the fighting, the shouting in your head. One side says eat because you are hungry and the other says no, you don't deserve to eat – you are greedy and look how fat you are! One side says sit down you are tired, the other says don't be so lazy, go for some exercise before you are allowed to eat a salad for lunch. The one side feels a cold coming on and wants to go to bed. The other side says no: punish yourself, fight through it, that's giving in. One side says buy yourself those gloves you need. The other side says no, just be cold, you don't deserve gloves... and so it goes on constantly, 24/7! This is what it is like. Day in, day out, no holidays, no rest, this is life with anorexia. This is living hell!

Seek Professional Help

What I would tell anyone out there in a similar situation or who knows someone who is, is this: get professional help as soon as the first signs appear. This is a potentially deadly disease. Contact one of the many organisations out there, such as Beat or FightED.

If someone thought they had cancer they would be away to the doctor and get tests. They would undergo all necessary treatment until they were diagnosed and treated. They would be surrounded openly by friends and family who would offer tea and sympathy. So why should someone with anorexia be any different? Because it is different – it is still totally misunderstood.

And just like someone who is terminally ill in a physical way, no one can really understand unless they have suffered the same illness, experienced the same symptoms and undergone the same treatment.

And what is even worse is that this is not an illness from which people openly admit to suffering. Sometimes sufferers are in denial, that is part of the problem. This illness, or any mental illness for that matter, doesn't often make light-hearted office chat. It is more seen with disdain, horror, and a complete lack of understanding!

Eating is such a normal part of life to most people that it is hard for them to imagine how someone could not want to eat, but would rather starve themselves. And in this way, the openness of such an illness becomes a taboo subject. And here lies one of the main issues. Until more people understand the illness and why it manifests itself in some people and not in others, the way ahead will continue to be paved with thorns for those struggling to come to terms with what it does to an individual, their lives and that of their nearest and dearest.

While the external symptoms and consequences of the illness are often clear for many, they do not see nor understand the internal workings and, sadly, that is where the real danger lies. To the innocent, confused bystander the solution is to eat more, but without understanding the consequences of that the goal of victory will not be easily won. It is the deep manifested mechanics of the illness that does the real damage, the mind games, the mental tricks that tell the sufferer lies about what type of person they are, how fat and greedy they look. And so the vicious circle continues until they no longer know or can see the real truth of how they are, what they look like or what they need to do to survive. Logic and rationality no longer exist. As the eating disorder takes hold, the mind becomes more twisted and with it the body more tortured. The sufferer no longer knows the truth!

I would not wish this illness on my worst enemy. So if this book does one thing by helping someone else it will have been worth it!

I have listed various sources of help, from books to websites to lifelines. There is a lot of support out there but you need to want help, first. That is the first step to a new happier, healthier life! I wish you every success.

Love Ali x

BIBLIOGRAPHY

Bashir, M. *Interview with Princess Diana. BBC1.* Retrieved February 1, 2012.

BBC Radio 4: World at One radio interview with Mark Austin, 29 November 2016

BBC News, 29 November 2016, *Newsreader Mark Austin reveals Daughter's anorexia Battle* http://www.bbc.co.uk/news/health-38146394

BBC News, 27 November 2016, 'We've travelled 8,000 miles to see our anorexic daughter', by Emma Forde, 5 Live Investigates:
http://www.bbc.co.uk/news/health-38121799

BBC News, 9 January 2017, *Mental health reforms to focus on young people, says PM:* http://www.bbc.co.uk/news/uk-politics-38548567

BBC News, 2 July 2014, *Anorexia treatment at Beechcroft Unit in Belfast criticized*

BBC News, 26 June 2017, *DUP-Tory deal: Where is the money going to be spent?*

Belfast Telegraph, 19 December 2015, *"Just go home and eat". GP's advice for eating disorder girl.*

Bemporad, J. R., (1996), *Self-starvation through the ages: Reflections on the pre-history of anorexia nervosa. International Journal of Eating Disorders*, 19: 217–237.

Brumberg, J. J., (2000). *Fasting Girls: The History of Anorexia Nervosa*. New York, NY: Vintage Books.

Channel 4, Mark Austin & Andrew Radford, 24 August 2017, *Wasting Away: The Truth About Anorexia.*

Coleman, R., (1994). *The Carpenters: The Untold Story. An Authorized Biography*. HarperCollins.

Engel, B Psy.D., Reiss, N.S., Ph.D., and Dombeck, M., Ph.D. Feb 2, 2007. *Historical Understandings* – (Mental Help website)

Fogarty, R., (2001). *Karen Carpenter: A Drummer Who Sang.* Modern Drummer Publications.

Gordon, R. A., (2000). *Eating Disorders: Anatomy of a Social Epidemic.* 2nd ed. Malden, MA: Blackwell Publishers Ltd.

Hepworth, J., (1999). *The Social Construction of Anorexia Nervosa.* Thousand Oaks, CA: *Sage* Publications Ltd.

Heywood, L., (1996). *Dedicated to Hunger: The Anorexic Aesthetic in Modern Culture.* Berkeley, CA: University of California Press.

Steinhausen, HC. (2002) *'The outcome of anorexia nervosa in the 20th century'*, American Journal of Psychiatry, 159(8), pp. 1284-1293.

The Independent, 15 February 2016. *Five times Mental Health Services were failed by the Conservative Government.*

The King's Fund, November 2015. Report, *"Mental Health under Pressure"*

Jacob, G., Genderen, H. V and Sebauer, L (2015). *Breaking Negative Thinking Patterns*

PricewaterhouseCoopers (February 2015) *'The Costs of Eating Disorders, Social, Health and Economic Impacts'*

The Telegraph, 1 October 2017, *Photoshopped images to come with a warning in France.*

The Telegraph, 19 April 2017, *Prince Harry: I sought counselling after 20 years of not thinking about the death of my mother, Diana, and two years of total chaos in my life.*

The Victoria Advocate (Victoria, Texas). March 12, 1983. Irregular Heartbeat Killed Singer. Retrieved 2015-06-03.

VH1, (1998) *Behind the Music: Carpenters.*

Vogler, R. J., (1993) *The Medicalization of Eating: Social Control in an Eating Disorders Clinic.* Greenwich, CT: Jai Press, Inc.

Young, J.E. and Klosko, J.S., (1993). *Reinventing Your Life.* Dutton, New York.

Young, J.E., Klosko, J.S., and Weishaar, M.E. (2003). *Schema Therapy: A practitioner's guide.* Guildford Press, New York.